Experiential Language Teaching Techniques

*Out-of-Class Activities for Learning
the Language and Culture of the United States*

Resource Handbook Number 3

edited by

Michael Jerald and Raymond C. Clark

illustrations by Patrick R. Moran

PRO LINGUA ASSOCIATES

Publishers

Published by Pro Lingua Associates
Brattleboro, Vermont 05301

SAN 216-0579

Library of Congress Cataloguing in Publication Data:

Main entry under title:

Experiential language teaching techniques.

    (Resource handbook/Pro Lingua Associates ; no. 3)
    Bibliography: p.
    1. English language--Study and teaching--Foreign
speakers.   2.   Activity   programs   in   education.
I. Jerald, Michael, 1942-   . II. Clark, Raymond C.,
1937-   . III. Series: Resource handbook ; no. 3.
PE1128.A2E94   1983   428'.007   83-3061

ISBN 0-86647-003-4

Printed in the United States of America

Acknowledgements

Many people have assisted in the writing and production of this book, and we are grateful for their contributions. Some of the techniques are the original idea of a particular individual. Others are variations of techniques that have been in common use for many years, and it is difficult to assign credit to any one person. The following people made direct contributions to this book:

Lisa Brodkey wrote "The Scavenger Hunt," an old camp game given a new life.

Andy Burrows developed "The License," and also wrote "Weekend Homestay," which is based on a concept originated by The Experiment in International Living.

Pam Helmick wrote this version of "Eating Out," a favorite activity of students and teachers at The School for International Training.

Alexis Johnson has made good use of "Errands" with dozens of her students.

Pat Moran wrote "The Observer," his own idea, and "Drop-Off," an old Peace Corps training exercise adapted for the purpose of language learning.

We also owe a debt of gratitude to three people who provided us with ideas. Francine Matarazzo Schumann created the "Dear Abby" technique. Her idea, in fact, is in our minds the original model for experiential language teaching activities. Some of Janie Duncan's work on the use of interviews for teaching ESL was incorporated by the editors into "The Interview" and "Man on the Street." Victor Miller first used the name "I Couldn't Help Noticing" for a different technique with a different purpose in a workshop at the Center for Theater Techniques in Education in Stratford, Connecticut.

There are others who helped by testing the techniques with their students and/or by offering ideas and suggestions for improvement: Jackie Blencowe, Rob Duncan, Jeanne Jensen, Frank Mausley, Steve Newman, Kevin O'Brien, Steve Robinson, Sally Smith, David Williams, and Andrew Willimetz.

Most of the typing was done by Elaine Malek-Madani, Cynthia Wiseman, and Marian Aldred, and their patience and good humor are particularly appreciated. Lisa Cook did the typesetting on The Experiment in International Living's IBM OS-6, and Andy Burrows designed the book and did the layout.

We would like to express special thanks to the many "native speakers" and "strangers" in the Brattleboro area who through the past several years have been accosted, interviewed, polled, queried and entertained by students on experiential learning missions. Their patience and goodwill has been unfailing. Al Lynch and the Foreign Language Department staff at Brattleboro Union High School have been most helpful in setting up and carrying out "School Visit." Gini Milkey, Director of the Windham County Retired Senior Volunteer Program, set up the exchange with the Senior Volunteers that served as the model for "Time Line." The Senior Volunteers themselves have been most helpful in carrying out the exchange, and finally, the waitresses at the Skyline Restaurant in Marlboro helped make "Eating Out" a successful and enjoyable activity.

And special thanks from MJ to John Schumann and Michael Hillmann for their efforts in the development of this type of learning strategy and for their encouragement and friendship throughout the past fourteen years.

Mike Jerald
Master of Arts in Teaching Program

Ray Clark
International Students of English Program

The School for International Training
Brattleboro, Vermont
January 1983

Table of Contents

Experiential Language Teaching Techniques

Dedicated to the Memory of

Alexander Lipson

Friend, Teacher, Inspiration

Introduction

This book is a collection of techniques for teachers who want to help their students bridge the gap between practicing the language in the controlled, secure environment of the classroom and using it for communication in the unpredictable real world just outside. Traditionally, the teacher's job ends at the classroom door, after many weeks of exercises, drills, role-plays, and dialogues. The students are then left on their own to take the final step of learning by using the language in culturally and socially acceptable ways. These techniques provide a way for the teacher to be part of the learning process from beginning to end.

Although they were written primarily for ESL students in the United States, these techniques, with just a little work on the teacher's part can be easily adapted for use in other English-speaking countries. By the same token, they can be used for teaching other languages in the countries where they are spoken, such as teaching French as a second language in France. Also, with a little more work and some creativity on the teacher's part the basic idea behind the techniques can be applied to the teaching of languages in places where they are not spoken, such as teaching German in the U.S. "Road Show" for example, was first used by Peace Corps trainees learning Farsi in Vermont.

We call them experiential techniques because the learning that takes place is based on and comes from field experiences that the students have, as opposed to being based on classroom activities. The teacher's job is to provide the structure for the experience, to prepare the students for going outside of the class, and to help them analyze what they have learned from it.

1

Introduction

At the heart of every technique are the excursions out of the classroom to perform a clearly defined and structured task that will bring the students in direct contact with the language and culture. The teacher prepares the students in class for the experience, sends them out to do the assignment on their own, and then helps them learn as much as they can from it when they return. The students will be able to use language and communication strategies already practiced in class outside in real situations; they will be exposed to new expressions, words, and grammatical items, and they will gain first-hand experiences with the culture. But most importantly, the students will gain confidence in their ability to function in American society.

The techniques are arranged not, as might be expected, by relative linguistic difficulty, although there is some correlation between the sequence of techniques and the linguistic proficiency of the students, but rather by the degree of risk involved for the students. In other words, the more intense and less controllable the contact with unknown native speakers is for the student, the higher the element of risk. Technique #1, "The Observer," for example, is a very low-risk technique because the students do not have to have direct contact with people to complete the exercise. Technique #13, "Eating Out" is somewhere in the middle, and Technique #26, "Time Line" is high-risk because it requires several open-ended conversations with the same person. In general then, any technique can be used with any proficiency level, although it is advisable to start beginners with low-risk activities.

We have found that the key to having these techniques work successfully for our students is in helping them to feel confident in their ability to control the linguistic and cultural aspects of the situations they will be in when performing these tasks. The fear of making mistakes in public, or worse yet, of totally losing control of a conversation can demoralize even the most highly motivated student. Some of the things we do to minimize this fear during the in-class preparation phase are:

2

Introduction

1. Help the students practice the questions they will ask, and help them anticipate and understand some of the answers they might hear.

2. Make sure they know appropriate ways, both linguistically and culturally, to get a person's attention and explain who they are and what they want.

3. Provide them with phrases and strategies that will help them control the conversation, like:

    I'm sorry, I didn't get that.
    Will you say that again, please?
    Before you go on, let me see if I've
       got that.

4. Go over appropriate ways to end a conversation after the students have gotten what they want. These of course, will vary according to the situation and could be a simple "Thanks," to someone on the street who has given directions, or "Thank you very much for your time," to somone who has been interviewed for half an hour.

5. Equip the students with "Escape Clauses" for the times when things do not go well, like not understanding a word of what a person is saying, or realizing that the person is going to ramble on forever. For example, here are some of the magic words that will allow a student to end almost any encounter politely in a way that the native speaker will understand:

    I'm sorry, I have to go.
    Oh (looking at watch)! I'm late for an
       appointment. I have to run.
    I'm sorry to interrupt, but I have to go
       back to class now. Thank you very much.

6. Give the students a pep-talk. Stress how they have all the tools they need to control the conversation. Emphasize the fun they will have, and encourage them to maintain their sense of humor.

Introduction

These techniques are not part of any particular language teaching approach or method. We see them as a collection of different tools for different purposes, and as such we do not expect anyone will use all twenty-eight of them. Rather, as with any tool, we expect you will choose those that will answer the needs of your students in the context of your situation. In a particular program, for example, you may use only one or two, but you might also find it worthwhile to use them several times.

One final note regarding the choice of personal pronouns we have made: In order to present a readable text uncluttered by such awkward eye-stoppers as he/she or (s)he, and in order to give equal recognition to both genders, we use feminine pronouns in odd-numbered techniques and masculine pronouns in the even-numbered ones.

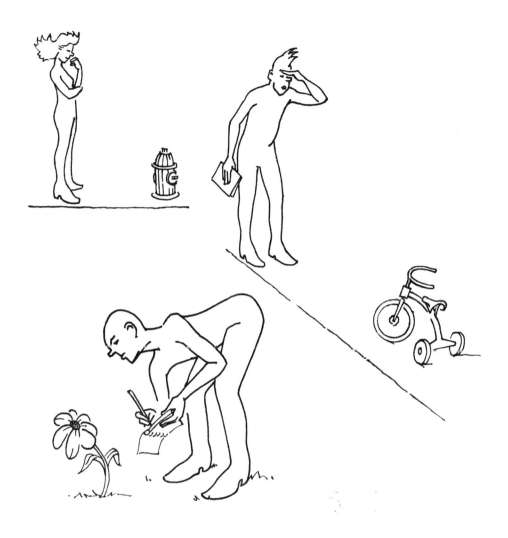

The Observer

Each student takes a brief excursion as an observer into the area immediately outside the classroom. Upon returning to the class, each student describes her observations.

The Observer

PURPOSE:

> This low-risk activity can be used to generate and provide practice with descriptive adjectives and structures (locatives, there is/are, comparatives, etc.) used in describing objects. It can be used early in the language program to begin developing an awareness of what is different in the new culture.

PREPARATION:

> 1. Explain to the students that they will take a 15-minute walk alone outside the classroom and that during their walk they must choose something to describe to the class when they return. Suggest they choose something that is different or not found in their home country.
>
> 2. Distribute a paper with a series of questions to elicit a detailed description of an object (see notes).
>
> 3. Explain the questions on the paper. The students brainstorm adjectives and expressions that can be used for description as you record them on the blackboard.

FIELD WORK:

> The students embark with their guideline questions and return at a specified time. Send them off in different directions to ensure that they work by themselves.

The Observer

BACK IN THE CLASSROOM:

1. Back from their excursions, the students review their notes and write a detailed description of the object. Circulate to check the students' work.

2. In pairs, the students read their descriptions to each other without naming the object. Through questioning, each student tries to guess what the other's object is.

3. In the large group, each student describes her object without referring to her written description. The other students guess what the object is.

4. Post the written descriptions on the blackboard for the students to study.

VARIATIONS:

1. The students can draw maps of their journeys and describe their itineraries to the class to practice directions.

2. To practice present habitual tense, the students can observe a workplace or business activity (a restaurant, post office, construction site, etc.) and describe how it functions.

3. The students can draw pictures of their objects. Post the drawings and have each student describe what she intended to convey. Other students discuss their reactions to the drawing.

4. Have the students write short poems describing their reactions to places or events encountered on their excursions.

5. Ask the students to describe how their objects reflect the culture, and how their objects differ from those in their own culture.

7

The Observer

NOTES:

1. It is important to stress the observer role to the students, encouraging them to look carefully at everything that crosses their path during their excursions--even suggesting that they remain silent and unobtrusive. This can relieve them of the anxiety of engaging in conversation and also help them sharpen their observation skills.

2. It is also helpful for students to understand the difference between observing and judging. Stress that the purpose of their field work is to gather objective, descriptive data about what they see. Later, in class, they will have the opportunity to analyze their observations and express opinions.

3. Any location outside the classroom can serve as an area for exploration: the campus grounds, the countryside, the city streets or the building where classes are being held--even their rooms.

4. Some questions for the students to answer in the field might be:

   How big is it?
   What shape is it?
   What color is it?
   How much does it weigh?
   Is it always this size, shape and color?
   Where is it usually found?
   Is it part of something else?
   Is it alive?
   Is it stationary?
   What does it look like?
   What is it used for?

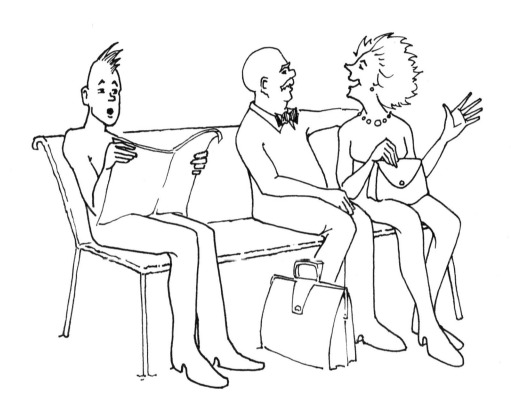

The Eavesdropper

The students, working alone or in pairs, find some
people conversing in public. They listen unnoticed,
take notes, and return to class.

The Eavesdropper

PURPOSE:

This low-risk activity gives the students an opportunity to see how Americans express themselves in common, everyday situations. It is structured so that the students can discover typical verbal and non-verbal strategies native speakers use to communicate with each other.

PREPARATION:

1. Give the students an overview of what they are about to do.

2. Make two lists on the board: the topics of conversation they might expect to hear, and the catch-words and phrases people use to move a conversation along, like "I know," "uh-huh," "you know what I mean." Have them tell as many as they can before you help.

3. Explain and demonstrate how gestures, body movement, distance, eye contact, posture, touching and tone of voice, are all part of communication and help convey the speaker's meaning.

4. Suggest nearby places where the students are likely to find people conversing in public, such as the school cafeteria, a park bench, a bus stop, a line at a theater, a department store, or on a bus or subway.

5. Help the students practice explaining who they are and what they are doing, in case someone asks them.

The Eavesdropper

FIELD WORK:

1. The students, working alone or in pairs, find some people they can listen to unobtrusively.

2. They take notes while listening. At this point, they should write only enough to help them remember the conversation later. They also are to observe the non-verbal strategies being used. Set a time limit for this stage.

3. Immediately after listening, the students find a place where they can sit and write as much of the conversation as they can remember.

4. The students return to class at the specified time.

BACK IN THE CLASSROOM:

1. The class discusses their general reaction to the experience. Some possible questions to focus the discussion are:

   a. How did you feel eavesdropping on someone?

   b. What did you do to overcome your fear?

   c. Did anything unexpected happen to you, such as someone asking you what you were doing? If so, how did you handle it?

   d. What new insights into U.S. culture have you gained? What new questions do you have?

2. Working alone, or with their field-partner if they had one, the students spend three minutes looking over and adding to their notes.

The Eavesdropper

3. Working in groups of five or six, the students give an oral summary of the conversation they heard. Then the class makes a combined list on a large piece of paper of the words or phrases they heard the most often and post the pieces of paper on the wall for all to see. Finally, they help each other understand what is on the papers, with assistance from the teacher.

4. When the students are telling how they felt doing the exercise, accept what they say non-judgementally. A response indicating that you heard and understood is all that is needed.

5. Following the same format as in 3, above, the students list and discuss the non-verbal aspects of communication they saw.

6. Each group prepares a five-minute skit using the data on their pieces of paper as a base. They write a dialogue, practice, and then perform it for the rest of the class. A variation of this, to highlight non-verbal communication, is for the students to speak their lines silently, as though they are on television and the volume is turned all the way down. The audience guesses the meaning based on the pantomime.

The Eavesdropper

VARIATIONS:

1. The students tape-record the conversation with an inconspicuous cassette recorder. Although more difficult to do, this variation provides an accurate sample of real speech for the students to analyze and practice. It is especially effective for advanced students.

2. After doing "The Eavesdropper" as described, the students actually enter into the conversation of the people they have been listening to. They listen long enough to understand the topic being discussed, and then join in by saying something like, "Excuse me, but I couldn't help hearing you mention last night's baseball game, and I'd like to ask you a question." This can be particularly useful for advanced students learning culturally appropriate ways for interrupting and expressing opinions.

NOTES:

1. In the preparation stage, it is more important to help the students become aware of what to listen and look for than it is to give an exhaustive list of everything they might hear or see.

2. Even though this is considered a low-risk activity, as it does not require direct contact with native speakers, it can be somewhat frightening due to the fear of getting "caught in the act." This makes step 5 in the preparation stage especially important for helping the students gain confidence in their ability to do the task successfully.

What Time Is It?

The students go out of the classroom and ask several people what time it is.

What Time Is It?

PURPOSE:

This activity is designed to help the students learn to understand and tell the time with a minimum of class time spent on it. It also serves as a model for students to use to teach themselves other similar routines.

PREPARATION:

1. Make two columns on the blackboard or on a piece of large paper. In the left-hand column make a list of two or three common phrases used for asking the time. In the other column, list the common ways for telling the time, on the hour, the half hour, and the quarter hour. Use what the students already know before adding information yourself. The list might look like this:

Ways to Ask	Possible Answers
What time is it, please?	It's five o'clock.
	Half past six.
Can you tell me the time, please?	Six thirty.
	A quarter to twelve.
Excuse me, do you have the time?	Eleven forty-five.
	Quarter past eight.
	Eight-fifteen.

2. Practice asking for the time and understanding common ways of telling it. For example:

Step 1. Students ask Teacher what time it is, using a pattern on the board.

Step 2. Teacher looks at her watch and says an arbitrary time, following one of the patterns on the board.

Step 3. Students write what they heard on paper.

What Time Is It?

Step 4. Teacher writes what she said on the board for students to compare with their answer. If the students need more practice, they can do this exercise again, in pairs.

3. Explain the routine the students are to follow outside the classroom. Explain that it is perfectly acceptable to ask the time of a stranger. There is very little risk involved.

FIELD WORK:

1. Each student goes out alone, through the building, down a street, into the park, or anywhere where she is likely to meet people.

2. The student looks at her watch to see what time it is, and then puts her watch away.

3. The student asks three or four people in a row what time it is. She listens to answers, says thank you, and moves on.

4. The student keeps asking the same question until she has gained confidence in approaching people and in asking the question. By this time she should also find it easy to understand the answers.

5. The students return to class after 10-15 minutes.

What Time Is It?

BACK IN THE CLASSROOM:

1. The students write down as many of the answers as they can remember. Spelling is not important at this stage. They should also describe any non-verbal answers, such as showing 10 fingers for 10 o'clock.

2. In small groups, the students compare answers, and help each other write them correctly.

3. One student at a time writes a different answer on the board.

4. The students ask questions about the list, add information or explain wherever necessary.

5. The students describe unusual things that happened to them. Help the students develop an awareness that what they may perceive as unusual may be a cultural difference.

VARIATIONS:

1. Once the students have done the exercise as described above, they will have had a lot of practice in producing the question "What time is it?" and hearing and understanding the answers. Now they are ready to produce variations. This can be done easily by turning the answers into questions, like this:

   Step 1.   Student looks at watch, sees the time.
   Step 2A.   Student stops someone and says, "Excuse me, is it 9:00?"
   Step 3.   Student will <u>hear</u> typical answers to a yes/no question, including informal, colloquial ways of answering like -- yup, uh huh, sure is, or a nod of the head.

What Time Is It?

Step 2B. By asking if it is the wrong time, e.g. asking if it's 10 o'clock when it's 9 o'clock, the student will elicit negative answers to the question and additional information such as, "Your watch must be slow," or "Is your watch broken?"

2. This exercise can serve as the basis for an investigation of cultural aspects of time in the U.S. Some openers might be: How do Americans value time? What expressions, e.g., "Time is money," do you know? What does "on time" really mean -- Ten minutes before the appointed time, or five minutes after? When are you late? Does it vary from business to social situations?

NOTES:

1. This is an excellent technique for helping the students gain confidence in going out and encountering strangers. Asking for the time only takes a second, and the student does not have to worry about the person asking her any questions she might not be able to answer.

2. This technique can be adapted for other kinds of rituals the students need to learn, such as "What's the date today?" or "Do you have change for a dollar?"

3. The first time the students do this exercise, it is not important for them to be able to say the time. They only need to know how to ask for the time and to recognize some common ways of saying the time.

4. A useful background reading for Variation 2 above, is "Making Sense Without Words" by Edward T. Hall, Jr. in Seymour Fersh, ed., Learning About Peoples and Cultures, p. 75.

Sign Language

The students "collect" signs from a walk down Main Street. They look for signs, write them down and bring them back to class for definition and discussion.

Sign Language

PURPOSE:

Getting around in a foreign culture can be greatly facilitiated if one understands the written messages that are available.

PREPARATION:

1. After explaining the nature and purpose of the activity, ask the students to contribute signs they have seen around town. Have someone write them on the board or a piece of large paper. This can be good spelling practice if one student dictates the word to the one writing it on the board.

2. Go over the list with the class to clarify any doubtful meanings.

3. Have the students categorize the signs. Some common categories might be:

   a. Advertisements
      1. Names--Carter's Little Liver Pills
      2. Phrases--Everything 1/2 off!
   b. Traffic and Safety Notices--Stop, Walk
   c. Regulations--No Parking
   d. Announcements--Closed for Renovations
   e. Information--Birthplace of Paul Bunyan
   f. Slogans--Put Litter Where it Belongs
   g. Place Names
      1. Streets--Flat Street
      2. Stores--The Book Cellar
   h. Miscellaneous

4. Divide the class into groups, each group being responsible for collecting signs in a particular category. Some categories are easier than others.

Sign Language

FIELD WORK:

1. The students go to town. Give them a reasonable amount of time to look for signs in their category and any different, interesting signs they have not seen before. No dictionaries.

2. Each group's goal is to find 10 to 20 signs in the assigned category. The students make sketches of the signs, note where they saw them and write any other information they think might be useful in determining the meanings and purposes of the signs.

BACK IN THE CLASSROOM:

1. The groups draw their signs and post them in the classroom.

2. The class looks over the signs and tries to understand their meanings. Dictionaries are permissible.

3. The students describe and talk about their signs while you serve as a resource.

4. Discuss the use of signs in the United States and compare this with the use of signs in other countries. (Also, see #4, under "Variations.")

5. Invite the students to tell of any new insights into American society and culture they may have gained by doing this exercise.

Sign Language

1. Analyze the grammar of signs. What kinds of words are left out? What verb forms are used? Study the prepositions. Distinguish generic names and brand names. Examine brand names for word-play, e.g., "Head 'n Shoulders Shampoo," "Sony Walkman," "Pepsodent," "Alpha Bits."

2. Re-write signs into full sentences, such as:

   Right Turn Only -- In this lane, only a right turn is permitted.

3. A drive along a highway will reveal a different set of signs from that found in town.

4. The class makes a large drawing of Main Street (or the area they have just explored), in which they include as many of the signs as possible. Put the drawing on the wall or bulletin board. Then, working in small groups (according to nationality if possible), the students make a similar "sign drawing" of a typical Main Street in their respective countries. This can serve as raw material for discussions about similarities and differences in the use of signs among all of the countries represented in the class.

5. After the town has been examined, send the students in groups to do an in-depth study of the signs in a particular place, such as a bus station, department store, bank, post office.

6. Have the class concentrate on collecting special kinds of signs, such as bumper stickers, T-shirt slogans, historical markers and plaques on buildings and monuments, gravestones, and for more advanced classes, graffiti.

7. Have your class sponsor a "T-Shirt Day" for your school. Everyone is encouraged to wear a T-shirt with a slogan. Have a contest to see who can write down the most T-shirt slogans and their meanings.

8. After the students have collected their 10 to 20 signs for their category, have them choose the one or two signs they find most puzzling and ask a native speaker to explain them.

NOTES:

1. Before the students go out to do the field work, it is helpful for them to be aware that signs in the U.S. are found in many more places than on the ends of posts or in store windows. For example, banners across streets, "vanity" license plates, merchandise labels and packaging, destination signs on buses, bumper stickers and T-shirts.

2. Instead of doing all the follow-up immediately (the sheer number of new signs can be overwhelming) do one category a day over a period of several days.

3. This exercise is particularly useful for literacy classes. Not only is it a low risk activity for the students, but it deals with reading at the survival level.

4. Among several books which use signs as the basis for language learning activities are:

   Greatsinger, Calvin, Signs Around Town, Syracuse: New Reader's Press, 1976.

   Huizenga, Jann, Looking at American Signs, Skokie, Illinois.: National Textbook Co.

   Richey, Jim, Sign Language (Books A, B, C, and D), Hayward, California: Janus, 1976.

Mapping It Out

Students go to a section of town with an incomplete street map. Their task is to label all streets and buildings that appear on the map.

Mapping It Out

PURPOSE:

This activity can be done early in the language program, even with beginners to acquaint them with the town and to get them out of the classroom and into the street rubbing shoulders with the natives.

PREPARATION:

1. Make an unlabeled street map of a nearby area. Prepare a copy for each student.

2. Hand out the map and give the assignment. Decide at this time if you will allow students to work in pairs or not.

3. Tell the students they have to fill in the map. Here you can give other guidelines such as, "You must put at least 25 labels on your map." You may want to build in other tasks that will require them to speak to native speakers, e.g. "You have to find out the business hours of every shop on Canal Street."

FIELD WORK:

1. Send out the students with a time deadline and clearly designated pick-up point (if necessary).

2. If this is one of their first "on the street" assignments, you might want to wander around being inconspicuously available to support or help.

BACK IN THE CLASSROOM:

1. On the board or on a large sheet of paper, draw a map similar to the one given to the students. This may be done beforehand.

2. Have the students give you the names for streets, buildings, landmarks, parks, etc. as you ask for them. To practice oral spelling, have them spell out the names.

3. Once the map has been filled in, practice locating places through a variety of questions and answers, e.g. "Where is the _____? It's next to _____."

4. Talk about the experience. Did they ask anyone for help? Did people ask them what they were doing? How does this place differ from similar places in their countries?

VARIATIONS:

1. The assignment can be done in two or three different locations: campus, town, a section of a city, a residential area.

2. In a larger town or city, assign each student a different sector. Then back in the class, put all the sectors together into a single large map.

3. Give the students a blank sheet of paper and have them draw the map from scratch. It would be best to prescribe some limits such as "The blocks limited by Main Street, High Street, Green Street and Elliot Street."

NOTES:

1. Post the completed map(s) in the classroom for future lessons such as techniques #6 "Where in the World," #7 "Road Show," #14 "Town Survey," #16 "Errands."

2. Not all students are skilled at understanding street maps, so an orientation to map reading may be necessary.

Where in the World?

The students go out of class and ask directions to some place in the area. They return to class after approximately 15 minutes and talk about what happened.

Where in the World?

PURPOSE:

Asking for and understanding directions is one of the first things someone has to do in a new place, but it is usually more complicated than "Where is..." and "It's...". The students need to understand the various ways native speakers actually give directions.

PREPARATION:

1. Have the students, working in pairs, look at a map of the area and choose a place they want to ask directions for. They will not actually go to the place as part of the exercise, so it does not have to be close to the classroom.

2. Write one or two common ways for asking directions on the board. Then, next to the questions, write a list of words and phrases commonly used to give directions.

Asking for Directions

Can you tell me the way to ____?
How do you get to ____?

Giving Directions

turn	to the left	corner	near
go	to the right	light	next to
walk	straight ahead	block	across from

3. Have the students, working with their original partners, use the map and the lists on the board to make educated guesses as to how directions to the place they have chosen would be given. It is not important that they be completely accurate, as they will not be giving the directions when they go out, only asking for them.

4. Set up a role-play requiring the students to ask and give directions to "their place," as part of a complete, culturally appropriate exchange:

Student 1:   Excuse me, can you tell me how to get to Fenway Park?

Student 2:   Sure, go down two more blocks and turn left at Kenmore Square. It's about three blocks ahead on the left.

Student 1:   Thank you very much.

Student 2:   That's OK. Good luck.

Student 1:   See you later.

Each student should play both roles several times. Circulate among the groups and help only where necessary. The object at this point is for the students to become fluent in asking for directions, and to recognize some of the answers when they hear them.

FIELD WORK:

1. The students leave the classroom in pairs and ask the first person they see for directions. Because the first time may be frightening, suggest that they just listen, say thank you and leave whether they understood or not.

2. The students continue to ask several other people for directions to the same place for about 15 minutes or until they gain confidence. Suggest that as their confidence increases, they ask various kinds of people in a variety of situations, such as men and women, young and old, adults and children, people standing still, walking fast, in stores or offices, or on buses.

3. The students take notes of words and phrases they hear, especially those that are new to them. They also note who said them and the situation they were in.

Where in the World?

BACK IN THE CLASSROOM:

1. In groups of four (two of the original pairs) the students list the words and phrases they heard. They then make a complete list on large paper or the blackboard.

2. Ask for questions about the list and help the students answer them. Add the category of gestures and help the students make an inventory of the gestures people used while giving them the directions.

3. Have the students discuss the cultural differences between giving directions in the U.S. and in their home countries.

4. For further linguistic practice, the students work in new pairs and role-play asking for directions to various places on the map, starting with the original places each had chosen.

5. Using American gestures only, the students give silent directions as you point to places on the map.

VARIATIONS:

1. After the students have gained confidence in asking for directions and in understanding the answers, they go out and practice saying the answers. They do this by putting the answers into the form of a question asking for confirmation. For example: "Is the post office three blocks straight ahead?" "Is this the way to the post office?" "Do I turn right at the light and walk through the park to get to the post office?"

2. They can elicit negative answers in the same way and discover common reactions to someone who has made a mistake. For example:

   "Is this the way to the post office?"
   (While walking in the opposite direction.)

   "Is the post office next to the Burger King on Elm Street?"
   (When the student knows it is not.)

3. The students go out alone and ask directions to a place that they really do not know the location of. This increases the risk, but at the same time, it increases the satisfaction of doing it successfully.

NOTES:

1. As this technique is particularly suitable for beginning students, it may be the first time many of them will be required to use English with strangers. If this is the case, then a "pep talk" might be helpful. Stress how they have all the tools they need to control the conversation. They know how to begin the conversation, and more importantly, they know the magic words to end the exchange politely and escape before they get in over their heads.

2. The idea behind having the students repeat the same questions over and over again is that it is a low-risk way for them to gain confidence in their ability to use the language with real, live people.

3. Knowing where the place is that they are asking directions to, especially the first time around, helps the students anticipate and more easily recognize the answers they will get. This, in turn, gives them courage to attempt what other-wise could be a frightening experience.

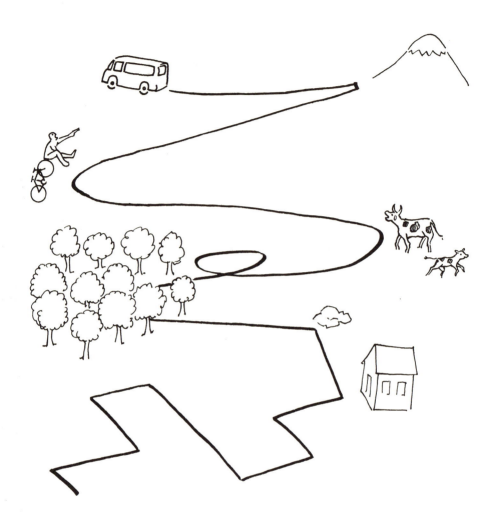

Road Show

The students and teacher all pile into the school van and the class is given a destination on a map. The class gives directions by referring to the map. The teacher drives, but cannot talk.

Road Show

PURPOSE:

The private automobile is not only the primary means of transportation in the U.S., it is in many ways the focus of American culture and an appropriate symbol of our times. Students of English need to be familiar with how the automobile has shaped and been shaped by American culture. A useful beginning is to learn to use roads and highways to find one's way around. This technique helps students learn how to read road maps, and how to ask for and give directions. It can also be used to introduce cultural discussions on the role of the automobile.

PREPARATION:

1. Hand out a map of the area and help students become familiar with the terminology needed for the exercise, e.g. "turn left," "go straight," "bear right," etc.

2. Practice directions by announcing to the class a starting point on the map, then whisper a destination to one student who gives directions while the others follow. When she is finished the "followers" state where they are.

3. Have the students practice asking questions for getting directions and explaining themselves, e.g., "I'm learning English, so I hope you won't mind if I write this down."

Road Show

FIELD WORK:

1. The teacher gets the school van and then gives each member of the class a map with a destination marked on it--or two or three destinations. In turn, each student must give a direction such as go straight, turn left, etc. A poorly constructed command "stalls" the car, but the teacher follows wrong directions if the English is correct. The result is much confusion to be sorted out.

2. The students write down all the road signs they see. They draw pictures of the signs and what the signs say.

3. Every so often, the teacher stops at a place where the students can ask directions. Each student takes at least one turn at getting out (alone) and asking directions to the destination, without the map in hand. Each student writes down the directions she receives. When she returns to the van, she tells the others what she learned and they check it with the map. If the directions do not agree with the map, the same student has to ask another person, until things get straightened out.

Road Show

BACK IN THE CLASSROOM:

1. The students retrace the route that was taken and restate the directions that were given, e.g., "Juan said, 'Take Third Street for two blocks,' then Maria said 'Turn left on Fourth Avenue.' "

2. The students write a narrative of the trip, or they write a dialogue in which they give directions to someone.

3. Collect all the signs that were seen and explain any they do not understand. Put them on a ditto stencil along with other words and phrases that were encountered during the trip.

4. The students write the directions they got from people they asked on a large piece of paper. Help them correct the language; then ask for observations about the different ways native speakers give directions.

5. In small groups, the students discuss their observations about what they saw and how the highway system differs from their home countries.

Road Show

VARIATIONS:

1. Go for a drive, without the students knowing the destination, and have the students take notes. Then when you get back have them recount the drive, e.g., we left the school at 2:45 and headed west along Black Mountain Road until ....

2. Have the students take notes on where they see people and what they are doing. Back in class, discuss how their notes compare with what happens in their own countries.

3. The students study other aspects of the automobile:

   a. An on-the-spot vocabulary lesson focusing on automobile parts.

   b. An "Operation," like starting the car. See Clark, Language Teaching Techniques, p. 25.

NOTES:

1. Insist on precise directions. For example, at a fork in the road, "bear left," not "turn left."

2. It is important that the students understand the directions before they get into the van.

3. Be clear about what "stalls" the car (see #1 under Field Work).

4. Make the directions challenging--lots of turns, so the students will not be bored.

5. A useful article for a follow-up discussion on the place of the automobile in American society is "The Sacred 'Rac'" by Patricia Hughes in the book Learning About Peoples and Cultures, Seymour Fersh, ed.

MTA

The metropolitan transportation system is explored
and mapped out by the class.

MTA

PURPOSE:

Getting around in a city can be difficult and expensive unless one is familiar with the bus or subway system. This technique will force the class to figure out how the system works (or doesn't work) so that "Take the A train" becomes a meaningful direction. In the process of trying to reach a destination the students will also be required to ask strangers for assistance and directions.

PREPARATION:

1. Obtain a map of the urban transportation system and plan out a separate itinerary for each member of the class. Try to put together a network of itineraries that will add up to a rather comprehensive exploration.

2. Write out the directions for each itinerary on separate slips of paper.

3. Explain the purpose of the exploration to the students. You can vary the guidelines according to the particular circumstances of your class and location, but a useful requirement is to have each student double-check his progress by asking at least one question on each leg of the trip. For example, some useful questions might be:

> "Excuse me, is this the bus to _____?"
>
> "I need to get off at _____, can you tell me when we get there?"
>
> "This is the outbound train to _____, isn't it?"

4. Hand out the itineraries and allow the students to study them - even memorize them - and work on pronunciation of place names.

5. As a group activity, go over useful phrases and words, such as:

> token
> transfer
> express
> I'm a stranger here, can you help me?
> I'm lost.

FIELD WORK:

1. Send the students off with sufficient change, plenty of encouragement and an emergency telephone number to call if they really do get lost. Give them a time limit, as well.

2. As the students carry out their assignments they should take notes on their itinerary, the responses to their questions and any other questions that occur to them as they ride along.

BACK IN THE CLASSROOM:

1. On the board or a large piece of paper, put an outline sketch of the area and key places the students travelled to.

2. As the students return, have them draw their itineraries on the outline map, labeling route numbers, stops, stations, etc., thereby producing a master map.

3. When everyone is back, go over the master map or, if available, hand out maps òf the metropolitan system. Check for accuracy and completeness.

4. Have each student describe his itinerary. Allow others to ask questions.

5. Talk about other questions, incidents and conversations that may have occurred as a result of the trips.

VARIATIONS:

1. Have the students travel in pairs, rather than individually.

2. Give the students additional assignments to carry out along the route to prove that they actually got to where they were going. For example, for each check-point or transfer along the route they have to find the answer to a question you have given them, such as "What's on the corner of 3rd and Main?" or "What color is the door of the Drug Fair on 17th and G?"

3. Give the students a list of things to do on the bus, such as listen in on conversations or ask people where the bus goes.

4. Throw in a "walking" problem. For example, "Get off the subway at City Square Station and walk to the bus stop on the corner of Federal and 3rd Street." This will force the students to ask for street directions.

5. Have everyone meet at the same central point for an end of activity social event.

NOTES:

1. Obviously, this technique will have to be varied according to the particularities of the local transportation system.

2. Avoid rush hours.

3. Also see technique #6, "Where in the World?"

SPECIAL VARIATION: "Magical Mystery Tour" (MMT)

In a non-urban setting, this technique can be done as a simulation. Get together with a few other teachers and plan out a simulated transportation system using your own cars and a few miles of local roads or streets. See the sketch below for a sample system that could be set up almost anywhere in a small town or campus. The system on the sketch map would be superimposed on the existing street system.

The students are not given the map. They are given only an itinerary. They must get off at each place on their itinerary and note a simulated (or real) street address. After everyone has completed his itinerary, the class re-assembles to do the back-in-class activities previously described.

The system below requires three cars and is set up in such a way that the students are forced to make transfers to get to certain points.

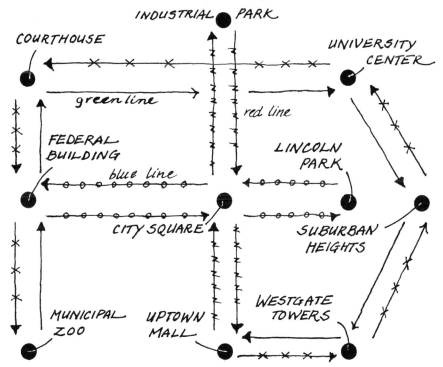

A sample itinerary for the system above, printed on a 3 x 5 card might be:

Start: City Square	3rd Stop: University Center
1st Stop: Industrial Park	4th Stop: Federal Building
2nd Stop: Uptown Mall	End: City Square

Supermarket

The students go shopping for the week's groceries. They do not actually purchase the items, but list them in their notebooks.

Supermarket

PURPOSE:

By trying to plan out the purchase of a week's groceries, the students will have to deal with food names, partitive expressions such as "a bottle of ____," the organization of a supermarket and comparative pricing.

PREPARATION:

1. Call a local supermarket to get permission to bring the class for a simulated shopping trip.

2. Explain the purpose of the exercise to the students.

3. Give the students the assignment: "You have $60.00. You need to buy the food for the next seven days for two people. Plan out your meals for each day."

4. Give them a list of additional supplies and staples that are also needed for this week. A few suggestions:

   a jar of mayonnaise   a bottle of bleach
   a roll of paper towels   a bottle of ketchup
   a pound of margarine   4 flashlight batteries
   a bag of flour   a bottle of cooking oil

5. As the students write their lists, help them with vocabulary.

6. Explain the way unit pricing works and tell them they have to record their purchases and that when the trip is over, a prize will be given to the best shopper, i.e. the person who buys good balanced meals for the least money.

Supermarket

FIELD WORK:

1. Upon arrival at the supermarket, have someone contact the manager to inform him of your arrival.

2. Give the class a time limit and turn them loose. Let them carry out their assignment without your coaching and support.

3. The students go through the aisles recording their "purchases" in their notebooks.

BACK IN THE CLASSROOM:

1. Compare results. Did anyone over-spend? Did anyone fail to buy seven day's worth of food? Who bought the most? etc.

2. Have one or two students put their lists on the board, or have them read them aloud slowly. Allow the other students to ask questions.

3. Ask the students to describe and label the various departments and sections of the super-market. Ask them where they would find certain items, e.g. "Where would I find floor wax?"

4. Work on other vocabulary and expressions that they encountered. This is a good exercise for working on names for containers and quantities.

5. Talk about grocery shopping in the U.S. as compared with their own countries.

44

Supermarket

VARIATIONS:

1. The students can work in pairs. This will require them to talk to each other.

2. Give them a question or questions to ask the attendants. Have them take notes on how they respond.

3. If you feel daring, have the students buy your groceries for the week.

4. Discuss food likes and dislikes. Use somebody's list as a basis. Read it and ask others to comment: "Would you buy this?" "Have you ever eaten this?"

5. Have the class buy the food for a class dinner which they will plan and prepare.

NOTES:

1. Pick a shopping hour that will be convenient for the store. The exercise could be hectic if the store is crowded.

2. The exercise doesn't require much contact with native speakers, but it could if you require the students to ask for help. At the same time, do not put too much of a burden on the other customers and attendants.

Scavenger Hunt

The students go out of the classroom to find all the items on a prepared list.

Scavenger Hunt

PURPOSE:

    This activity gets the students out of the class-room to ask questions, learn or practice vocabulary, and become more familiar with the immediate environment.

PREPARATION:

1. Prepare a list of 10-15 items that may be found in the environment outside the classroom. The items can be small objects or pieces of information or a combination of both. Refer to Notes section for some ideas.

2. Explain to the class that they will be given a list of items to collect from the surrounding area. They are to collect all the items, or as many as possible, and return with them to the classroom by a designated time.

3. If competition is involved, explain that the first person to return with a complete assortment of items will be the winner.

4. Lay out any ground rules desired: whether or not dictionaries or telephones may be used; any areas such as dorms that are off-limits.

5. Hand out the lists (each student gets the same list) and set a deadline for returning to class.

FIELD WORK:

    The students leave the classroom with their lists to collect the items called for.

Scavenger Hunt

BACK IN THE CLASSROOM:

1. "Check in" each person and his collection as the class returns. Determine a "winner," if any.

2. Review the vocabulary involved, double-checking that all items are understood.

3. The students write a narration of what happened or make a tape describing the activity.

VARIATIONS:

1. This activity can be done in pairs or teams.

2. The students can identify certain things, but not bring them back. For example,

   > What's painted on the wall next to the soda machine?

   > Whose office is across the hall from Bobbi's?

   > What are three things visible in the pond?

3. For a more challenging "hunt" the students can be given a list that requires them to speak to several people. For example: Find (and name) people who:

   a. have travelled to Kenya.
   b. have eaten octopus.
   c. have flown in a glider.
   d. have climbed Mount Washington.
   e. cannot swim.

4. Make up a list of objects and information that will require the students to canvass the immediate neigborhood, going from door to door to collect their items. Help them with useful phrases such as:

   > I'm a student on a scavenger hunt. Do you have a ____?
   > May I take it to class?
   > Do you want it back?

Scavenger Hunt

NOTES:

1. Finding information is somewhat more difficult than finding items. First, the student must take a greater risk if communication with a native speaker is required. Secondly, the activity may require a little research in an almanac or encyclopedia.

2. Some sample lists might include:

   a. Objects (nouns)   (adjectives)

1. a twig	1. something red
2. a maple leaf	2. something long
3. some moss	3. something sharp
4. a piece of bark	4. something crooked
5. 3 pebbles	5. something soft
6. 2 pinecones	6. something crunchy
7. an old newspaper	7. something shiny
8. a beer can	8. something brittle

   b. Information

   1. ___(name) 's___ birthday
   2. something which is ___(name)'s___ favorite color
   3. a driver's license from ___(state)___
   4. the color of ___(name)'s___ eyes
   5. the date ___(country)___ became independent
   6. how many teeth a baboon has
   7. how many windows are in ___(local building)___
   8. what time a local movie begins
   9. how much a cup of coffee at ___(local coffee shop)___ costs

The Thing

Using an object (the Thing) as a focus, each student engages native speakers in a conversation to elicit information about the object.

The Thing

PURPOSE:

This activity gives language learners an opportunity to approach native speakers and engage them in a limited conversation which the students can control. The students will not only gain confidence, they will also have a chance to expand their vocabulary and practice eliciting factual, cultural and even personal information from a native speaker.

PREPARATION:

1. Select a variety of objects that are portable and suitable for this activity. The objects should be relatively simple but also have sufficient conversational potential. See Notes for a few ideas.

2. Explain the technique to the students. They will receive an object which will be their Thing. They have to take their Thing to two or three native speakers and with their help put together a 60-second monologue about the Thing that will be presented to the rest of the class.

3. Hand out the Things to the students.

4. Go over a list of questions that will be helpful. For example:

> What's this?
> What's this part called?
> What's it used for?
> Who uses it?
> Why do they use it?
> When do they use it?
> Where can I buy this thing?
> How much does it cost?
> Do you like this thing?
> What things are similar to this thing?

5. The students can practice with each other to warm up for the field work.

The Thing

FIELD WORK:

1. Send the students out, armed with their Things, their notebooks and dictionaries.

2. Each student should talk with at least two and preferably three people to collect enough information to give a 60-second monologue.

3. The students should take notes. After they have done their talking, they write out their presentation. This should produce a one-page composition.

BACK IN THE CLASSROOM:

1. In turns, the students show their classmates their objects and give a 60-second monologue.

2. After each presentation, stop for questions and answers.

3. Listen for interesting, useful and new vocabulary and write a few words on the board after each presentation.

4. When everyone is finished they can exchange Things two or three times and try to talk about each other's objects. The words on the board may be practiced at this time.

5. Finally, discuss the process of collecting the information. What was easy, difficult, fun, irritating, etc. Why? How can this experience help them become better language learners?

6. Collect the compositions and check them for accuracy.

The Thing

VARIATIONS:

1. Instead of having the students do oral presentations have them write their presentations on a ditto. Run off a copy for everybody and then go over each one as a group, making corrections.

2. Back in the class they can work in groups of three or four to make their presentations.

3. Give everybody the same object and see how much variation in answers there will be.

4. Instead of you choosing the objects, tell the students to choose any object that for them is typical of American culture. Before the Field Work, have them tell the class (or write) why their object is typically American. When they return, they can compare their answer with those of the people they interviewed.

NOTES:

1. Some Things might be:

a frisbee	a fishing reel
a small house plant	a fruit or vegetable
a mouse trap	a candy bar
a cassette tape	a shirt or jacket
a stapler	a cigarette lighter
a baseball	a wallet
a disposable razor	a flashlight
a light bulb	an umbrella
a pocket calculator	a bag of potato chips

2. An interesting reading, after doing this activity, is "Interpreting a Foreign Culture: the Nacirema" by Horace Miner in Seymour Fersh, ed., Learning About Peoples and Cultures.

3. For ideas on how to help the students prepare their monologues, see "Spiel" in Clark, Language Teaching Techniques.

Be the Expert

The students learn the English necessary to explain and demonstrate something they already know how to do.

Be the Expert

PURPOSE:

Sitting down with a native-speaker in a one-on-one situation can be a frustrating experience if the conversation gets out of control. One way for the student to maintain control is to talk about something he is familiar with. For beginners and for students who are just beginning to engage in solo field experiences, it is helpful to focus the conversation on something that is concrete, rather than abstract. This activity allows the student to control a conversation by talking about something that is both familiar and concrete.

PREPARATION:

1. Ask the students to list some skills that they enjoy doing. Explain the nature of the skills you are looking for, and give some examples from your own inventory. For example:

    I can read music.
    play softball.
    identify songbirds.
    read topographical maps.
    use a card catalogue in a library.

2. After the students have made a list of their own skills, have them read their lists to each other.

3. Select one skill for each student. There are three options here: You choose one, the student chooses his own, or the student's classmates request one.

4. Explain the assignment: "Find a native speaker who has some knowledge of your skill. Ask the native speaker to help you explain and demonstrate your skill."

5. Give the students tips on where and how they can locate an appropriate person to work with.

Be the Expert

FIELD WORK:

1. The students locate a helper.

2. With the helper they collect the words and phrases that are needed to describe the skill to another person.

3. Individually, the students go over their notes and practice presenting their skill.

BACK IN THE CLASSROOM:

1. One at a time, perhaps over a period of several days, the students present their skills to each other.

2. After each presentation allow time for questions and discussions.

3. Talk about the process of eliciting information from an informant and controlling the conversation. Collect useful phrases, such as,

> "Say that again, please."
> "Did you say ____?"
> "What is the word for this _____?"

VARIATIONS:

1. Give each student a ditto stencil and have him prepare a hand-out to go along with his presentations.

2. Allow the students to bring their helpers to class to re-enact the field experience.

3. Students who have similar skills can work together as a pair. This might be especially useful if the skill is complicated.

4. Some presentations can be done outside the classroom, e.g. changing the oil and filter in a car. This is a good opportunity for some free labor if your car needs an oil change.

NOTES:

Some ideas for skills:

    a. Using a piece of equipment

        a camera
        an automobile
        a mini-computer
        a microfilm reader
        a movie projecter

    b. A physical activity

        playing a sport
        doing close order drill
        martial arts
        calisthenics

    c. A process

        reading a map
        doing a square root
        sign language
        filling out a form
        developing film

    d. Playing a game

        poker, bridge, etc.
        a board game
        a party game

    e. Manual skills

        making sketches
        origami
        paper and scissors activities
        tying knots
        sewing

Eating Out

The students and teacher go to a restaurant and enjoy breakfast together.

Eating Out

PURPOSE:

Going to a restaurant provides the students with actual practice of vocabulary, phrases, and appropriate cultural behavior for eating out. Sharing a meal together is also a good ice-breaker and lets the students and teacher get to know one another on an informal basis. This in turn helps develop a sense of class unity.

PREPARATION:

1. Before the outing, the students are introduced to the vocabulary and phrases which they are likely to need in ordering breakfast at a restaurant. For example: "over easy," "seconds," "a refill." If possible, obtain copies of the menu beforehand as a source for vocabulary.

2. Use the menu as a prop in restaurant role-plays.

3. Discuss the cultural aspects of dining out. This may include how to get the attention of the waitress politely, tipping, paying, and even a description of certain regional foods (maple syrup, grits).

FIELD WORK:

Enjoy the food and the company. This is a good time for informal conversation, as well as an opportunity to use new phrases and vocabulary. It should be fun!

Eating Out

BACK IN THE CLASSROOM:

1. The students write descriptions of the experience, including their impressions and what was seen and done along the way. These can be individual reports or a group effort written at the blackboard.

2. Using the class composition, the students then take turns reading parts of it into a tape recorder as a pronunciation exercise.

3. Discuss American restaurants. Ask the students how they differ from their home countries. Have them put together a list of "Does and Don'ts" for dining out in America.

VARIATIONS:

1. The students record their experience directly on tape with no written preparation. This can be replayed as an exercise in self-correction or as a dictation.

2. The students and teacher can simply discuss the experience. The students might compare it to dining out in their own countries. Discuss the similarities and differences and any specific cultural observations.

3. Before arriving at the restaurant, the students may be given specific tasks to perform while there. One student can be asked to make the reservations, another to lead the group into the restaurant and deal with the host or hostess. Someone else might explain whether the tab is "all together" or "separate checks". Have a student ask if there are seconds on the coffee.

Eating Out

1. Any meal may be selected for the outing. Breakfast is nice because it doesn't require spending a large amount of money. A student may order only a cup of coffee and still be comfortably a part of the group. Also, it is a great way to start the day!

2. Let the students carry out all the transactions at the restaurant. Provide them with questions or assignments, but let them deal with strangers for the answers.

SPECIAL VARIATION: "EATING IN"

The students and teacher decide on a place such as the teacher's home or the school kitchen where they can prepare and eat a meal together. The students take the responsibility for shopping for the ingredients and cooking the meal. The students are usually delighted at the opportunity to get away from the school cafeteria and to share dishes from their own countries. This is also a good way to build class unity.

See technique #9, "Supermarket" for some ideas on shopping.

Town Survey

The students spread out around town with specific assignments to learn about one place in detail. Later they return to class and create a mini-guidebook for the town or a section of the city.

PURPOSE:

This is a particularly useful and enjoyable
activity for students to do at the beginning of a
program. It helps them get to know a broad
spectrum of the community quickly, to get to
know their classmates by working with them, and
it provides them with an opportunity to speak
English in a real situation right from the
beginning.

Town Survey

PREPARATION:

1. Show the students a map of the city you are in. Ask them to identify the landmarks and areas they already know. Point out others they will need to know to do the exercise.

2. Explain the general idea of what they are going to do.

3. Put the students in groups of two or three. Give each group an assignment, consisting of a place to go to and a list of questions. For example:

   Go to the Rexall Drug Store, 39 Main Street.

   1. Who is the manager?
   2. How many people work there?
   3. What are their jobs?
   4. What do they sell?
   5. How do you get medicine?
   6. What's a prescription?
   7. How much are vaporizers?
   8. Is this the same as a drugstore in your country? How? How is it different?
   9. Buy one thing that costs less than $1.00 that you have never seen before. Find out what it is and what it's used for and bring it back to class.

4. Help students learn words and phrases they think they need to know. Have them role-play the situation and write a brief dialogue of the way they think the conversation will go.

5. Go over appropriate ways to start and end the conversation.

Town Survey

FIELD WORK:

1. The students go to their assigned places with their "task force" to complete the task. If it is feasible, they can practice asking for directions as in technique #6, "Where in the World?"

2. Before returning to class, the students take time to write down as many of the answers as they can remember.

BACK IN THE CLASSROOM:

1. Give the students a Reaction Sheet to fill out, based on the experience. For example:

   New words and expressions I heard:

   Words which caused problems:
       a)   problems for me:
       b)   problems for my listener:

   I wish I could have said:

   I expected that _____ would happen and:

   I was surprised by:

   Something funny that happened to me was:

   Next time I will:

2. Use the Reaction Sheet as the basis for small group or full-class sharing. Make a composite new-word inventory on a piece of large paper.

3. Each student shows the object he bought and explains what it is for.

4. Each group writes a dialogue based on what really happened. Then they compare it with the one they wrote in the preparation stage.

5. Each task force writes up a description of the place they went to and the services rendered. Enough copies are made so that everyone gets a complete set.

Town Survey

VARIATIONS:

> This technique can be used in conjunction with "Mapping It Out." The information gathered about the individual places can be added to the master map. If the students have already made the map, it can be used in the Preparation phase.

NOTES:

1. Assign the places the students will explore so that they cover a wide variety of places and services. Some general categories to keep in mind are:

   > Education
   > Recreation
   > Entertainment
   > Restaurants
   > Businesses
   > Social Services
   > Professional Services
   > Government
   > Religion

2. To gain the maximum benefit, the students in each task force should share the responsibility of asking questions. Before they leave the classroom, have each of them choose the questions he will ask.

Interview

The students interview people at the school or in the immediate neighborhood about a particular topic chosen beforehand. The interviews are pre-arranged by the teacher.

Interview

The very nature of an interview makes it an excellent low-risk, high-gain activity for language learning. It is a pre-arranged conversation between two people in which, by mutual agreement, one person asks questions and the other answers them. This activity is designed, then, to provide a structured experience in which the students can practice listening, speaking, and note-taking skills with native speakers they do not know. In addition, the students are learning general interviewing skills which are at the heart of many of the techniques in this book.

PREPARATION:

1. A few days before you do this activity, find volunteers at your school or nearby places to be interviewed by your students. Make the necessary arrangements and explanations. Some possibilities are office workers, school administrators, and shopkeepers. Try to find people your students are not likely to know.

2. Explain the activity to the students and describe what an interview is. It is important for them to understand how they will be able to control the conversation through the interview process itself.

3. Assign a topic or let the students choose one. The first time it might work better if you assign everyone the same topic. Some suggested topics appear in the Notes section.

4. With the students, brainstorm a list of words and phrases they anticipate needing for their interviews. Write them on the board or a large piece of paper.

5. Each student writes a brief dialogue based on what she expects will be said in the interview. In small groups the students can role-play each other's dialogues.

6. The students practice saying phrases they can use to check their understanding and to slow down the conversation when they feel overwhelmed. For example:

> I'm sorry, will you say that again?
>
> Sorry, I didn't hear you, will you please repeat that?
>
> Did you say that ...?
>
> Now, if I understand you correctly, you're saying that...

FIELD WORK:

1. The students conduct their interviews. Give them the name and address of the interviewee and directions.

2. During the interview the students take notes. They should ask for permission first, however.

Interview

BACK IN THE CLASSROOM:

1. The students give brief reports on how things went. Focus this discussion on feelings--Were you scared? Embarrassed? Confused? How did it end?

2. The students re-write the dialogues they wrote in the preparation stage, making them more accurate according to what actually happened. They make a list of the words and phrases they learned and of those that were new for them.

3. Make a list of "tricks" (verbal and non-verbal) the students used to win the person's confidence, to interrupt, to bring a wandering discourse back to the point. This can be the beginning of a class-produced interviewing handbook.

4. The students write thank you notes to their interviewees, mentioning specific points that were discussed in the interviews.

VARIATIONS:

1. The interviews can be conducted by phone.

2. Because of the moderate amount of risk involved in doing this activity, it is a good one for students to do alone. There may be a time, however, when you have to send them out in pairs or small groups, such as when you cannot find enough interviewees. In such cases, have the students divide up the responsibility for asking the questions equally before leaving the classroom.

Interview

NOTES:

1. Although it may not be apparent from the description, this technique can be used with students of all levels. The key is to assign topics that the students are familiar with and have practiced discussing in class. So for example, a beginning student can conduct a brief interview in which she asks only three or four biographical questions.

2. Some suggested topics:

   Family
   Job
   Hobbies and Pastimes
   Travel
   Religion
   Politics
   Current Events
   Social Issues

Errands

The students go out of the class and do real errands
for the teacher.

Errands

Being independent and taking care of oneself is a basic American cultural value and is an important part of living in the United States. An important part of taking care of oneself is being able to accomplish such routine, daily tasks as making a bank withdrawal, dropping film off to be developed, mailing a package, and making theater reservations. This technique is designed to help students learn how to overcome the fear and frustration of doing errands, thereby taking care of themselves in a culturally acceptable way.

PREPARATION:

1. Students set up a diagram or map of the town (or a few streets of a city) using the blackboard, colored rods, or pictures. Add buildings, name them and talk about what people do in them. Keep a vocabulary list on the board or on a large piece of paper.

2. The students role-play situations, building by building. Give each group a specific task to accomplish, such as getting a sweater dry-cleaned and a grease stain removed.

3. Build a list of polite and appropriate questions that students can expect to hear and say, for example:

> Can
> May   I help you?
> Could
>
> Can
> Could   you help me?

73

Errands

4. Give each student a card with an errand written on it. Include specific instructions and any necessary material. For example:

> Take these books to the Brooks Library on Main Street. Pay the overdue charges and renew ____. Take out ____. Ask the librarian for help if you can't find it.

For this example, you would give the student the books, the money to pay the fines, and your library card.

5. Give the students a time by which they must be back in class.

FIELD WORK:

1. The students go out (or are driven downtown) with their instructions and materials.

2. They perform their tasks and return to class.

BACK IN THE CLASSROOM:

1. Each student reports on the errand and gives the information learned. This report can be tape-recorded so that the teacher can work individually with error correction and pronunciation later.

2. The students help each other learn the new vocabulary, and they compile a list.

3. The students discuss the linguistic and cultural differences between the way these errands are done in the U.S. and their home countries.

Errands

1. While the students are doing the errands, they get information about the places where they are. In the library for example, include questions on the instruction card you give the student, like "What goes on in the library in addition to loaning books?" "Are there programs open to the public?" "Do they show movies?"

2. The students are sent to various buildings other than those where they might usually do an errand to find out what goes on in them. Similarly, they can investigate organizations such as the Chamber of Commerce and the Rotary Club.

3. After the students have finished their errands, they meet at a restaurant they have never been to. This gives them the added challenge of finding the meeting place. Coffee or ice cream for all, on the teacher, can be their reward for doing your errands.

NOTES:

1. This exercise works for beginners as well as intermediate and advanced students. Adjust the complexity of the errands to fit your students' abilities.

2. Consider the students' personal interests and needs when assigning the errands.

3. Some possible errands:

   a. Post Office. Students buy stamps, mail letters or packages, buy a money order, or get a passport application. Have them find out the cost of mailing something overseas. If the student is a stamp collector, have him ask about plate blocks and first-day covers.

Errands

b.   Dry Cleaners.   Leave   something   to   be
cleaned. Pick up something. Ask if they
can   remove   a   certain   kind   of   stain   from
suede, or some similar question. Find out
about storage services and other services
they may offer.

c.   Police Station.   Pick up a driver's manual,
pay a parking fine, ask directions, get a
bicycle license.

d.   Department Store. Buy something. Return
or exchange something.   Find the cheapest
price   in   town   for   something   you   are
thinking of buying (comparison shopping).
Find out how to open a charge account.
See   if   the   store   has   your   size   in   a
particular piece of clothing.

e.   Paying Bills.   Give the student a bill that
needs to be paid and a check.   Ask him to
bring back a receipt.

f.   A Bank.   Make   a   deposit   or   withdrawal.
Cash   a   check. Find out how to open a
savings account.   Find out which bank pays
the   most   interest   or   has   the   cheapest
checking account in town.

g.   And so forth...whatever you come up with,
the more real the errand is, the more responsible the student feels in doing it and
the more he will learn.   That which the
student readily puts off doing for himself
will be done gladly for the teacher.

The License

This activity is done in two phases: first, the students research the process of getting a license or permit, and then they apply for and actually get one.

The License

PURPOSE:

The main objective is for the students to develop the skills and confidence needed to obtain a license or permit. They will have to ask questions and understand answers in a bureaucratic setting, and fill out forms and follow procedures. They will also learn which licenses are needed for living in American society, the relative difficulty or ease in getting them, and they will gain some insight into how Americans view government regulations.

PHASE I

PREPARATION:

1. Explain what a license is and give examples of what they are needed for in the U.S. List the licenses the students already know about and add others they may not know of, such as driver's, hunting, fishing, dog, pilot, bicycle.

2. The students choose one license they want to get.

3. The class makes a list of what they think they will need to say in the offices they are going to. Help with vocabulary and phrases.

4. In pairs, the students role-play, asking for information about the license they have chosen. They include greetings and leave-takings appropriate to the anticipated situation.

78

The License

FIELD WORK:

The students go to the offices and find out how to get the license. Their objective is to leave the office with a <u>clear</u> idea of everything they have to do to get the license. They return to class with the information and the appropriate forms.

BACK IN THE CLASSROOM:

1. The students tell the rest of the class where they went and one thing that happened that they found interesting or unusual. Make a list for use later. This is to give everybody a general idea of everybody else's experience.

2. The students, working alone, write answers to:

   "What new words and phrases did you hear?"

   "What couldn't you say that you wanted to?"

   "What did you have trouble understanding?"

   Then, in small groups, the students compare their answers. Later, with the full class, answer any questions still unanswered.

4. The students read the forms and instruction sheets they brought back.

5. Working in pairs, with different licenses, each student explains to her partner the procedure for getting the license.

The License

PREPARATION:

1. The students fill out the forms. Check their work.

2. The students practice the language they anticipate needing to use, as in steps 3 and 4 of Phase I preparation.

3. Check each student's forms carefully and determine if they are ready to go out. For some students, individual meetings for further help may be needed to give them the confidence to go out and actually do the task.

4. Ask each student for a schedule of what they plan to do and when.

FIELD WORK:

The students take their forms to the appropriate office and go through the process of obtaining the license.

BACK IN THE CLASSROOM:

1. Follow steps 1 and 2 of Phase I, Back-in-the-Classroom activities.

2. Have the students show the licenses they have gotten and tell the class what happened in the process. The students listen, take notes, and write a summary of the procedure for each license. Schedule one or two such presentations a day until all have been given.

3. As part of these presentations, have the students tell how one obtains the same or similar license in their home country. Use this as the basis for a discussion of cultural differences.

The License

VARIATIONS:

1. The students get the information over the telephone instead of going in person. This is more challenging in some ways, but may be necessary in cases where there is not enough time or the office is too far. Another possibility is for them to write a letter requesting the information.

2. After the students have done Phases I and II, they can conduct a simulation exercise for other classes, or if this is not feasible, for each other.

3. In addition to getting licenses, the students may be interested in learning how to apply for other things that require filling out forms, such as credit cards, loans, visas and work permits.

4. Give the class a topic for a discussion or debate, such as "Why do we need licenses?" or "Living with red tape."

NOTES:

1. During Phase I of the Field Work, encourage the students to go alone. If they go in pairs, tell them both people have to talk.

2. Some licenses require an examination. In this case, make the preparation for the exam part of the lesson.

3. With the students going off in so many different directions, it is helpful to keep a chart of who is doing what, and when they plan to do it.

Sorry, Wrong Number

The students practice using the telephone to get information from a variety of businesses and agencies.

Sorry, Wrong Number

PURPOSE:

Using the telephone in a foreign country can be a terrifying experience. Although the instrument itself looks just like the one back home, everything about using it is different. It is even more baffling for those who have never used a phone. And in the U.S., being able to use a phone effectively is a basic survival skill.

This activity is designed to help the student of English gain some control over the phone and to use it comfortably for getting what he needs. The students will practice such skills as using the phone book, dialing local and long distance numbers, dealing with operators, and opening and closing conversations. They will learn how to communicate without the aid of visual clues such as facial expressions and gestures.

PREPARATION:

1. Go over the vocabulary associated with the telephone. Handout a list and have the students try to define the terms. Some suggested vocabulary items are:

dial	area code
receiver	telephone number
call	extension
dial tone	information
busy signal	yellow pages
station to station	white pages
person to person	directory
telephone bill	collect
long distance	direct dialing
operator	pay phone

Sorry, Wrong Number

2. Present basic ways of opening and closing telephone conversations. Give the students a sample dialogue for both a personal call and a business call. For example:

Business Call

Opening

A (Callee): Seymour Opticians, good morning.

B (Caller): Hello. I'd like some information about...

Closing

B: Well, thank you very much for your help.

A: You're welcome. Goodbye.

B: Goodbye.

Personal Call

Opening

A: Hello.

B: Hello, Bill?

A: Yeh?

B: Hi. This is Bob Smith. How are you?

A: Fine, Bob, how are you?

B: Fine. I'm calling to ask...

Closing

B: Well, OK. I've got to go now. See you later.

A: OK. Take care.

3. Give each student a card containing a task to complete, using the telephone, or give the same task to two or three people so they can work together. For example:

   Call People's Bus Lines and ask:
   - a) Do you go to Keene?
   - b) How much is the fare?
   - c) The departure and arrival times for next Friday? Are they different from Sundays?
   - d) Can I bring my bicycle? My dog?

4. The students write a dialogue for their task, based on what they think will be said, including openers and closers. Help with vocabulary and spelling, but do not change the substance of what they write. Part of the experience is for them to practice predicting what native speakers will say in a given situation.

5. Role-play the dialogues in pairs, sitting back-to-back. This is to simulate a real telephone conversation in which neither gestures nor facial expressions can be used for assistance in figuring out the meaning.

6. One student volunteers to make his call with the whole class watching. Take the class to a phone--in an office, or a nearby pay phone--and have the student make his call. The observers take notes. Tape the conversation if possible for better analysis in class later. If they are reluctant to volunteer, then you do it once, to set a model.

7. Send the students out to make their calls, or assign them to be done before the next class.

Sorry, Wrong Number

FIELD WORK:

1. The students find a phone and perform their tasks. For the sake of confidence building, tell the students to perform the same task, with different people, over and over until they feel comfortable doing it, and they can understand what people are saying.

2. After each call, the students take notes about what was said and how they felt doing it.

BACK IN THE CLASSROOM:

1. The students write down what was said, in dialogue form, and compare it with the dialogue they wrote before making the phone calls. Ask what was the same; what was different. What new words did they hear?

2. Discuss how they felt. Scared? Nervous? Did this change as they repeated the activity? What tricks did they learn for controlling the conversations?

3. Add other ways, based on this experience, of opening and closing phone conversations.

4. The students tell each other how people in their home countries use the phone.

VARIATIONS:

1. Give the students a list of names of businesses and individuals and have them find the numbers in the phone book (both yellow and white pages). Give them some names in other states, and in other countries to find through the operator.

2. Ask them to call the operator and find out how to make a collect call, and how to charge a call to a third number.

Sorry, Wrong Number

3. To practice hearing how people respond to someone who has called the wrong number, the students can call a business for information that the business cannot possibly know, or call a private phone (just pick one out of the phone book at random) and ask for someone you know will not be there.

NOTES:

1. Some places the students can call for information to practice their telephone English:

> Theaters
> Bus, train, planes
> Travel agencies
> Stores
> Car Dealers
> Banks
> Town/City Hall
> 800 numbers
> Dial-a-Joke, Dial-A-Prayer, etc.
> Want ads
> Classified ads
> Immigration Service

2. Assign the exercise several times, so that each student gets practice with several items on the list.

3. Tape-recording the conversations is very helpful for later use in class or for individual practice outside of class. Electronics stores sell an inexpensive device for connecting a tape recorder to the phone with a suction cup.

4. To help inspire confidence, point out that they can always hang up if things get out of control.

5. If necessary, do a preparatory lesson on spelling names orally and saying and understanding long numbers.

School Visit

The students visit a local secondary school where each student follows an American counterpart through the school-day schedule.

School Visit

PURPOSE:

Many ESL students enter the American school system near the end-point as university students. This activity introduces the students to the secondary school experience that American college students have come from. Even for ESL students not going on to college, a taste of the American secondary school experience can be a worthwhile cultural experience. By spending a school day with a young American, the students can also work on current idioms and slang. In many cases the shared experience leads on to invitations for more shared experiences after school and on the weekends.

PREPARATION:

1. The details have to be worked out first with the local school. The foreign language department is a good place to start, and even though not all your students may be speakers of Spanish, French or German, the cross-cultural contact alone can still be worthwhile for the American foreign language student.

2. After explaining the purpose and details of the visit, explain the U.S. educational system to the class and invite them to compare it with their own systems. A useful, simplified chart can be found in The ESL Miscellany, p. 206.

3. Ask the students to pay particular attention to and listen for the things American teenagers talk about, and the slang and expressions they use.

4. Finally, have the class prepare a list of questions that they would like to have answers to. Try to collect some information questions, such as "Do you have religion classes?" and some questions that deal with the opinions and attitudes of American teen-agers, such as "Do you think prayer should be allowed in school?" It is a good idea to ditto the list of questions and have each student carry them with her to the school.

FIELD WORK:

1. Bring the students to the school and have them pair off to spend the day together.

2. If it has been some time since you have been in a secondary school, it might be a good idea to follow one of the foreign language teachers through her day.

3. The students bring notebooks and record their observations and questions. They also collect words and phrases that they hear repeatedly, and find answers for their list of questions.

BACK IN THE CLASSROOM:

1. Have the students describe what they did and saw. At this point insist on non-judgmental observations.

2. Once everybody has described what they did, have them each contribute two or three "Why" questions.

3. Try to answer the questions and lead the students toward understanding what they have seen before they make value judgments.

4. Have the class construct two lists: the pros and cons of what they saw. This should lead into a discussion.

5. After discussing the education system, go over any words and phrases the students may have collected, and discuss the answers they have collected from their questionnaires.

6. The students write thank-you notes to their hosts.

VARIATIONS:

If possible, invite the American students to spend part of a day with your class. Have your guests join in with some games where even with their superior knowledge of English, they cannot dominate the activity. Try "Matched Pairs" or "Who's Who" in Index Card Games for ESL. You can also pair students up and let them walk around the campus for an hour. Another activity is to try to decipher the lyrics from some current rock hit. It may be comforting for the ESL students to discover that even American teenagers cannot figure out what is being said.

NOTES:

Sometimes following somebody else around for five hours can be tiring and boring. For this reason, some kind of observation guide or list of questions is useful not only for directing and sharpening observation, but also for giving the student something to do while seated in a class that may be boring or difficult to follow.

Dear Abby

The students read a typical advice to the lovelorn letter, go out and ask native speakers how they would answer it, and then return to class to compare answers.

Dear Abby

PURPOSE:

> The students are exposed to a variety of current views on common social issues. They also have the opportunity to investigate the language used in talking about personal problems without talking about their own problems.

PREPARATION:

1. Choose an advice to the lovelorn letter from a newspaper, make a copy for each student, without the columnist's answer.

2. Explain what these columns are, show examples, and ask the students if they have them in their own countries.

3. Help the students <u>understand</u> the letter. In small groups they read and discuss the meaning of the letter, and answer each other's questions, but they do not answer the question posed in the letter at this time. Answer any other questions the students cannot answer for themselves.

4. To prepare for their encounter with native speakers, the students brainstorm sentences and phrases they can use to explain what they are doing, to introduce themselves, and to express thanks. Write them on the board.

5. Have the students role-play, if necessary, to build confidence in their ability to do the task.

Dear Abby

FIELD WORK:

1. The students go out to ask one to three native speakers (depending on the time available) how they would answer the letter. They take notes about the answer and about the background of the person who is answering.

2. Set a time limit. Ten to fifteen minutes for each person to be interviewed is usually enough.

BACK IN THE CLASS:

1. In small groups, the students tell each other the responses they got to the letter. They help each other write their answers concisely and clearly on the board or a piece of large paper.

2. The students read all the answers. Help them with comprehension and new vocabulary.

3. Ask the students to comment on the answers. Are they all the same? Are they different? Why? How are they representative of U.S. culture?

4. Have the students compare the answers they got from Americans with what someone in their own country might say. A leading question might be: "How would your mother, or best friend, or teacher answer the question in the letter?"

Dear Abby

VARIATIONS:

1. The students discuss things that happened while they were doing the interviews. Ask them to focus on reactions and responses that they found surprising or unusual.

2. Have the students write their own letters to a columnist, either individually or as a group.

3. The students can write letters to each other asking for advice.

4. Discuss other ways people give and get advice in America.

NOTES:

1. Send the students out individually, if possible; otherwise send them in pairs if they seem to be reluctant to do the exercise alone.

2. This activity can be repeated often, with different letters, without losing its freshness and usefulness.

3. Not giving the students the columnist's answer at the beginning makes the exercise more interesting. You can show them the answer at the end, but it may be anti-climatic. In fact, they may even forget to ask.

4. Sometimes it expedites matters to give the students the names and addresses of likely prospects to talk to. Then they can go directly to the person, and not waste time thinking of where to go. Also, this will help you ensure that they talk to a cross section of age, social and economic groups.

5. The idea for this technique is Francine Matarazzo Schumann's and was described by John Schumann in On TESOL '74.

The Joker

The students practice telling jokes in class. Then they go outside and tell a joke to a native speaker.

The Joker

PURPOSE:

Being able to tell a joke in a foreign language and have it work can be a very rewarding experience. It can provide insight into the culture and give one something more to say in social situations than "Isn't the weather nice." Students also get practice in disciplining themselves to speak clearly and with appropriate intonation and stress.

PREPARATION:

1. For several days preceding the Field Work, the students bring in jokes they have heard or read (not jokes they have translated from their own language). Write them on large paper or another place where they can be saved. Help the students understand them.

2. Help the students analyze the jokes that have been collected. What words and phrases appear frequently? Are there any common topics or themes? What makes them funny? To whom might you tell them? To whom would you not tell them?

3. The students choose one joke from the list and practice telling it in small groups. They criticize (coach) each other, until they can each tell their joke smoothly and with appropriate timing and emphasis.

4. The teacher helps the students come up with strategies for finding someone to tell their jokes to. The students brainstorm ways to get someone's attention, introduce themselves and explain what they are doing.

The Joker

FIELD WORK:

1. The students go out and tell their joke to a native speaker or preferably, a group of native speakers.

2. They are told to keep telling it, to different people, until they get a good laugh. When they bomb, tell them to ask the listener how to make it funnier.

BACK IN THE CLASSROOM:

1. In small groups, the students tell each other what happened.

2. Each group reports to the whole class. Focus the reports by posing three questions: 1) What unusual or funny things happened? 2) When the joke worked, why do you think it did? 3) When it did not work, why not?

3. The students write out their jokes. Circulate to check the work and encourage the students to help each other. The students post their jokes so that all can see and make copies if they wish.

VARIATIONS:

1. The students call Dial-A-Joke in New York, and record and transcribe the joke of the day.

2. The class writes its own joke book: a collection of the best jokes they have learned during the program. This can lead to a class publishing project to give to other students in the school.

3. The students submit jokes on a regular basis to the school newspaper.

4. The students translate jokes from their native languages and adapt and modify where necessary to make them work with native speakers. The students discuss how humor differs from culture to culture. Why is something funny in one country and not in another? Are there any universal joke forms or themes?

NOTES:

1. This can be a lot of fun if the students take the exercise and themselves lightly. Have them practice phrases like these, to be said with an impish grin and twinkle in their eye:

> I am a student of jokes. Will you help me please?

> I am learning to tell jokes in English. Will you be my straight-man?

> Would you like to do something silly with me?

> Would you like to help me make a fool of myself in English?

2. The Field Work for this exercise may take more time than you have during a class period. During lunch is an alternative, or as an overnight or over the weekend assignment.

3. The first time you do this exercise have the students tell the same joke to several different people until they can tell it smoothly, effectively, and with confidence.

Getting a Handle on Idioms

Current idioms are collected and analyzed in class by the students. On a regular basis, the students go outside of class, use them in a conversation with native speakers, and then return to class to analyze the results.

Getting a Handle on Idioms

PURPOSE:

One of the hardest things for any non-native speaker to master is the appropriate use of idioms. Being able to understand and use them correctly is essential for any student who wants to fit into a wide range of social settings--idioms are the essence of colloquial language. Books with lists are of some help, but they do not reflect current usage or allow for regional variations.

PREPARATION:

1. From the beginning of the course, systematically collect idioms the students hear outside of class. At the beginning of each class spend a few minutes asking the students what new ones they have heard since the last class and write them on large pieces of paper taped to the wall.

2. Help the students understand the meaning and the appropriate usage of each one as you write it. Have them keep an Idiom Journal. For each idiom they have four columns of information, arranged in a grid, like this:

IDIOM	MEANING	WHEN TO USE AND WITH WHOM	CAUTIONARY NOTES
YOU BET!	I AGREE! I WILL!	INFORMALLY WITH ALMOST ANYONE	DON'T USE IN FORMAL WRITING
RIGHT ON!	OK I AGREE! LET'S DO IT!	VERY INFORMAL WITH YOUNG PEOPLE	USE WITH FRIENDS

3. After there are ten or so on the list, have each student pick one to listen for and practice outside of the classroom.

4. The students practice saying their idioms to each other, in pairs, and then to the whole class. This is to gain confidence in saying them smoothly and clearly. Attention to pronunciation, intonation and stress is important at this point.

5. Check to be sure the students know the meaning and have a general idea of the appropriate usage of their idioms.

6. The students brainstorm ways they can work their idioms into a conversation. Help when necessary.

FIELD WORK:

1. The students go out of the class and use their idiom in a conversation with a native speaker.

2. The students take notes after each time they use the idiom. They note new words they heard and the reaction of the person they spoke to. Tell them to look for non-verbal gestures which give clues as to how they were received. Check the reaction of the person they used the idiom with. Did they wrinkle their face? Raise their eyebrows? Smile? What do you think these expressions meant?

Getting a Handle on Idioms

BACK IN THE CLASSROOM:

1. The students give a brief summary of what happened when they used their idioms. Look for humorous, confusing, or upsetting incidents that may have been caused by cultural misunderstandings. Use these as the focus of a discussion of cross-cultural differences.

2. Using their notes, the students reconstruct in writing the part of the conversation in which they tried out their idiom. They answer questions like, what was the sentence you used the first time you used the idiom? What did the person say? What did they do? Was their reaction unusual in any way?

3. Working in pairs, the students check each other's descriptions for clarity and grammatical correctness. Help where needed.

4. Have each student write one new word or phrase he learned from doing the exercise and one word or phrase he still is unsure of, on the board. Lead the class in helping each other learn the meanings of the words they do not understand.

5. The students add new information to their Idiom Journals.

Getting a Handle on Idioms

VARIATIONS:

1. This same technique can be used for learning rituals and common routines such as greetings, leave takings, ways of starting and ending conversa tions, paying compliments and making introductions. When collecting the phrases and recording them on the lists, it is especially important to help the students learn how to choose appropriate utterances for the people and situations they are in. For example, "Catch you later" is an appropriate way to say good-bye to a peer after class, but probably not to a doctor on the first visit to his office.

2. Students can take the initiative in collecting the idioms. Instead of waiting to hear them spoken, they can go out and interview people. For example, they might ask three or four native speakers how they would say hello in the morning to a) their children, or students, b) their spouse, or best friend, c) a stranger they meet in an elevator.

NOTES:

1. Sometimes it helps shy students to pretend they are someone else while doing the task. Tell them they are on a secret mission to infiltrate ordinary everyday conversations. It is a mission known only to them, and if they pretend to be cool, no one else will know.

2. This is a good activity to do regularly--for example, every weekend. This will "force" the students to have some contact with native speakers, and it will give you some fresh material to work with on Monday morning.

3. The first time the students do this, have them choose just one expression to work with. Then gradually have them increase the number to three or four at a time.

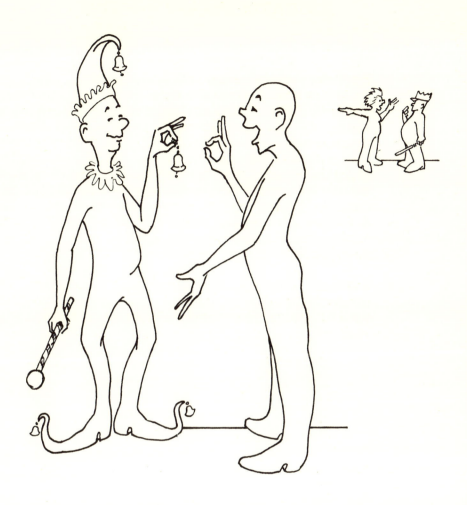

I Couldn't Help Noticing

The students practice both giving and receiving compliments in class, and then do it with native speakers outside class.

I Couldn't Help Noticing

PURPOSE:

English, unlike many other languages, does not have invariable rituals that everyone uses consistently for handling common social situations such as offering congratulations, expressing condolences, accepting a gift, and apologizing. This technique is designed to help English students learn how to give and receive compliments in culturally appropriate ways. It also can be used as a model for devising other activities for similar social rituals.

PREPARATION:

1. Explain what a compliment is and ask the students if they have heard any in English, spoken by native speakers. Write them down on a chart.

> Compliment:
> Response:
> Who said it:
> Who received it:
> Place:
> Circumstances:

2. Tell the students to listen for compliments outside of class. On a regular basis, spend a few minutes adding new ones to the chart and adding new information to those already there.

3. The students choose compliments and responses from the chart and practice giving and receiving them. In a role-play situation, the students practice making choices appropriate for use with various people in different situations.

4. Explain the field-work part of the activity. Then have the class write a brief dialogue which they can use to interrupt someone politely and pay them a compliment about some article of clothing or some object people commonly carry with them. An effective and easy opening line is: Excuse me, I couldn't help noticing that....

5. Finally, in the context of a cocktail party, the students can practice by milling around and paying each other real compliments about their clothes or personal belongings. Afterwards, answer any questions that came up.

FIELD WORK:

1. The students look for a situation in which they can compliment someone. It could be at mealtime in the school cafeteria, at a party, or even in public places, such as a bus stop. They give the same or similar compliment to at least three people. Give the students two or three days to carry out the assignment.

2. After each encounter, the students write down what they said, what the reply was, and any unusual or unexpected things that happened.

BACK IN THE CLASSROOM:

1. Whenever a student completes the field work she writes a one-page letter to another student in the class if she were a close friend back home. In the letter she describes the interesting experience: what she did, the words and phrases she learned, something unexpected that happened, and something funny that happened.

2. The letters are "mailed" through you. You add a little authenticity and fun to the exercise by playing the role of mail carrier with a flourish: "Ah, Fritz, it looks as if you have a letter. How nice. And here's one for you too, Carmen!"

3. The students give an oral summary of the letter they received: "I just got a letter from my friend who is studying English in ___." Yesterday she went up to a total stranger and ...."

4. Discuss the similarities and differences between the role and place of compliments in American society and the students' home countries.

I Couldn't Help Noticing

VARIATIONS:

1. After the students feel confident giving compliments for articles of clothing and personal possessions, they can try the more challenging task of complimenting someone for the way they do something or for their personal appearance.

2. The opposite of a compliment is an insult, and although you may not want to teach your students how to be insulting in English, it is useful for them to know how to express displeasure with another person's behavior. The use of humor is an acceptable and useful way of expressing displeasure. With advanced students you can explore the use of humor in classroom role-plays.

3. Another useful function this technique can be used with is asking for permission to smoke or asking someone to refrain from smoking.

NOTES:

Many other social situations requiring ritualistic phrases can be done in class as role-plays. Some possibilities are:

   introductions
   apologies
   invitations
   gift-giving
   condolences
   dining
   dating

Man on the Street

In the tradition of the Roving Reporter and the Inquiring Photographer, the students go out with a notebook and pen in hand and ask people on the street for their opinions about current social and political issues. Afterwards they return to the class to analyze the experience.

Man on the Street

PURPOSE:

This technique, another variation of the Interview, allows the students the opportunity to practice such skills as getting a stranger's attention, winning his trust, asking questions, and listening to and understanding opinions. The students also become familiar with current issues that are of concern to the local community.

PREPARATION:

1. The teacher and students choose a topic of social and political significance for the on-the-street interviews. Some preliminary preparation activities for identifying topics are reading a local newspaper every day for a week or two, and attending city council meetings.

2. Discuss the topic and the basic issues in it. Formulate a question that captures the essence of the issue and that the students can understand (see Notes, item 1).

3. Brainstorm a list of words and phrases the students might hear in the answers. It is not necessary that they be able to say them--only recognize them when heard.

4. The students practice asking the question and giving the answers in a role-play situation. They also can practice taking notes by writing down the answers their partners give and then checking for accuracy.

5. Help them think of effective and culturally appropriate ways to approach people and gain their cooperation. For example:

> Always use polite forms of address, like sir, ma'am, young lady, young man.
>
> Get people's attention first; then explain who you are and what you're doing; ask if they'll cooperate; then, and only then, ask your question.
>
> Show your school ID card.
>
> If someone doesn't want to answer, let them walk away; don't be a pest, and don't take it personally.
>
> A smile and a friendly look will help put people at ease.
>
> Be fast, ask your question, get the answer and go on; don't take advantage of people's good will by not letting them go.

FIELD WORK:

1. Send the students out to do the questioning. Tell them to return at a specified time and give them a minimum number of people they have to talk to.

2. The students work in pairs to ask their questions.

3. During the interviews, they write down the complete answer to the best of their abilities.

Man on the Street

BACK IN THE CLASSROOM:

1. Discuss what happened, especially unusual or puzzling things.

2. The students make oral summaries of the answers they got to the question. Put a composite list on the board or piece of large paper. Make sure everyone understands the list; then have the students look for common themes.

3. The students tell whether the issue would be relevant in their hometown, and if so how their father or mother might answer the question, and if their younger brother or sister would answer it differently.

4. Each interviewing team chooses what they consider the most interesting answer and writes it neatly on a piece of paper. After mistakes have been corrected, all of the papers are posted on the wall for all to read and ask questions about.

Man on the Street

VARIATIONS:

1. Have each pair of students choose a different topic to poll people on. Then when they come back to class, the students will have a variety of topics to share information on and learn about.

2. Volunteer to have your class conduct a real survey for the Chamber of Commerce, city government, or some other local organization.

3. Instead of simply being a newspaper reporter or "Gallup Pollster," the students can go all the way and take a camera (Polaroid-type is best) and tape recorder or video-tape recorder. The pictures and tapes can be used for compiling a collection of these interviews for publication in the school or local paper or broadcast on a local radio station or television station.

4. Gaining confidence with these brief encounters on a street corner can be the start of the students doing serious, in-depth interviewing of people about their daily lives, in the manner of Studs Terkel. A compilation of interviews can be made into a magazine as a class project.

NOTES:

1. The questions cannot be too trivial or too esoteric. They must be easy to say, easy to understand, and be answerable in about fifty words.

2. The first time out, it is helpful to assign each pair of students to a particular location. Choose places where they are likely to find a lot of people.

3. This activity can be done over and over. As long as the topics are fresh, it will be interesting for the students.

Solo

Each student chooses a place in the community that she wants to know something about. She then plans a visit, prepares for it, visits the place and then reports on what she found.

Solo

PURPOSE:

> Field trips are an important activity for every class, but it is unlikely that each student will have the opportunity to visit a place she is personally interested in, i.e. a trip to the fire station may be fun for most folks, but not everybody is turned on by red trucks. This activity allows each student to investigate a place that is of personal interest. It also requires the student to function alone to set up and carry out the trip.

PREPARATION:

1. Explain to the class that they are going to have a field trip next week to X different places (X = the number of students in the class).

2. Have them list places or areas in the community that they would like to learn about. Give a few suggestions yourself, if necessary.

3. As you elicit responses, begin planning who is going to go where. If two students want to visit the same place, try to get one of them to choose another place.

4. Summarize the destinations for the field trip, for example:

   > Juan is going to visit the Toyota dealer.
   >
   > Ann is going to visit the bank.
   >
   > Yoshi is going to visit the police station.

5. Next, give the details for date, time and transportation, for example, "I'll get the school van and we'll leave at 9:00 next Tuesday. Plan to spend about one hour at your site."

6. Tell the students that in the next few days they will have to call to arrange for their visit. Help them plan out how to call and make arrangements. See "Sorry, Wrong Number" for some ideas.

7. Finally, explain that they should also think about and plan out what kinds of questions they will need to ask, so that they can come back to class and be an expert on the purpose, structure, functions and personnel of the place they will visit.

FIELD WORK:

1. The students plan and carry out their telephone calls.

2. Once they have made an arrangement they will inform you they are ready.

3. On the appointed day the students visit their assigned places, armed with questions and a notebook.

BACK IN THE CLASSROOM:

1. When the visit is completed they will write up a report on their trip, and submit it to you for checking.

2. Over the next several days have each student give a 15-minute report on her trip.

3. As each report is given, encourage others in the class to ask questions or make comparisons: "In my country, we do it this way...."

Solo

VARIATIONS:

1. This assignment can also be carried out by pairs or small groups of students.

2. The field can be narrowed to stores, or agencies, or professional offices, or governmental services. So the opening question might be: "What kind of store interests you?"

3. The students can do this activity entirely outside regular class time.

4. To make the activity a little easier, the students could be asked to visit someplace they already know about.

NOTES:

1. This technique is similar to "Be the Expert" and "Town Survey," but somewhat more challenging. It could be a good follow-up activity after the students have done one or both of the others.

2. Working with the telephone and the Yellow Pages should be a prerequisite to this activity.

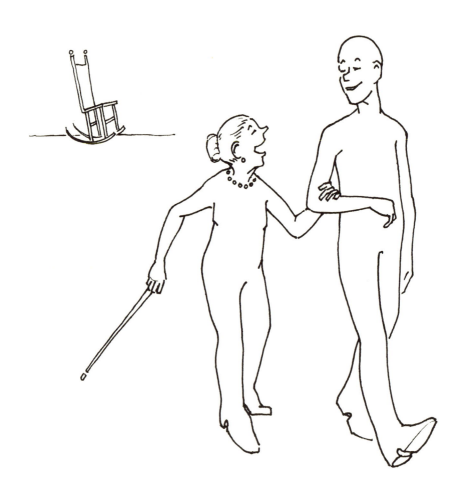

Time Line

The students meet regularly with older people to learn something about local history and the recent past.

Time Line

PURPOSE:

Foreign students can see American culture as it exists around them in the contemporary world, but they have not grown up in America and had the benefit of listening to grandfathers or grandmothers saying "Now when I was young we would...." This technique brings the students in contact with older people, an age group they do not normally deal with, and it gives the students an opportunity to learn a little of the history that underlies the contemporary people, places and things on Main Street.

PREPARATION:

1. Contact the Retired Senior Volunteer Program or the Senior Center to set up a series of visits, pairing each student with an older person as a partner. Although this technique will have some value as a one-time activity, it works much better if it can be done on a regular basis over several weeks.

2. Discuss the purpose of the activity with the students. It may be helpful to have someone from RSVP or the Senior Center come to the class to discuss the role of older people in American society.

3. A useful way to structure this activity is to put an 80-year timeline on the blackboard. The line will cover the lifetime of most of the participants. Then, have the students fill in significant historical events on the line. It might look like this:

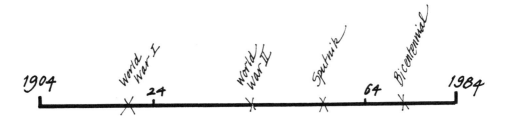

4. Tell the students that their objective is to write a biography of their older partner, placing him on the time line above.

5. Go over useful phrases with the students. For example:

> What was it like ...?
>
> How old were you when ...?
>
> What did you do before ...? (TV, etc.)
>
> Did you ever ...?
>
> Tell me something about ....

FIELD WORK:

1. The students and their partners meet once a week. For best results the sessions should be one to two hours in length and at least weekly over a four to six week period.

2. The first session may be used just for socializing. The student can also use this first session to introduce the assignment and discuss it with his partner. The student should also try to find out if his partner has things he would like to talk about or share.

3. Short strolls around town or a walk to a nearby park bench can be incorporated into the meetings.

4. The student should use his discretion in deciding how and when to take notes. If he does not take notes during the session, he should write up his notes immediately after the meeting while the conversation is still fresh in his mind.

5. At the conclusion of the visits the student writes a biography of his partner.

Time Line

BACK IN THE CLASSROOM:

1. Brief weekly discussions follow-up each visit. The discussion starts off with "How's it going?"

2. At the conclusion of the visits the students hand in their biographies. They can put them all together on ditto stencils for everyone to have.

3. Final discussions can focus on:

   a. local history.

   b. history as a key to understanding the present.

   c. the place of older people in American society.

   d. social and historical cross-cultural comparisons.

   e. how to learn language through face-to-face encounters.

VARIATIONS:

1. Instead of focusing on the life of the older person, the sessions can be about the history of the town--if the person is a long-time resident.

2. The class can do supplementary work on local history. Among the possible activities are:

   a. Visits to the local museum and historical society.

   b. Readings on local history. Back issues of the local newspaper would be a good source.

   c. A visit to a cemetary and other historical memorials and sites.

3. The students can do parallel time lines for their own country and compare them with the American time line.

4. Each student can write an autobiography and give it to his partner at the conclusion of the visits.

5. The class makes a collection of all the biographies and presents a copy to each of the partners.

6. Have the students include photographs of their partner in their report. Both current ones taken by the student and old ones supplied by the partner, are appropriate.

NOTES:

1. Although this technique can be done during class-time, it can also be done after class hours. In this case, it could also be an optional activity.

2. The older person might be able to come to the classroom and although this can be useful, the technique has more impact if it is done off-campus in the "real" world.

3. A nice way to say thanks to the people who helped out is to invite them to lunch or a school activity.

Weekend Homestay

After defining their expectations, the students spend a weekend in an American home. Back in class they assess their "homestay" and share what they have learned.

Weekend Homestay

PURPOSE:

Making friends, getting away from the grind, and being entertained American-style for a weekend are all worthwhile experiences for an ESL student. Providing a framework for this experience will also increase the students' understanding of American culture and self-awareness, and may even heighten their enjoyment.

PREPARATION:

1. Set up the weekend homestays. See Notes.

2. A day or so before the weekend homestay, ask the students to share what they know of their plans. Where are they going? How are they getting there? Have they been in contact with "their family?" What do they know about them? Put this up on large paper for future reference.

3. On a large piece of paper, help the students list their <u>expectations</u> of what living with an American family will be like. This is a time for them to express their concerns about the experience and to talk about preconceived views they have of American family life. Invite students who have had previous homestays in the U.S. or who have had homestay guests in their own homes to share insights.

4. Also make a collective list of the students' <u>objectives</u> to give them an idea of the range of things they can get out of the experience. Most of the objectives will fall into one of these categories: personal, "I want to have fun and eat well"; linguistic, "I want to practice idioms"; or, cultural, "I want to see how Americans discipline their children." Put these three categories across the top of the large piece of paper to serve as a guide for the students.

5. Using these two lists as resources, have each student write her own personal list of expectations and objectives for the homestay.

124

Weekend Homestay

FIELD WORK:

1. During the weekend the students should relax and have fun; this exercise should not be a chore. They should feel free to ask lots of questions, but they should also observe in detail (a) how their hosts live and (b) how they themselves react. Emphasize that they should try to notice and remember what they see and hear rather than to pass judgment on it. "My family ate when they were hungry and never sat down together" rather than "I (don't) like the way...!" Tell them to be "amateur anthropologists" as well as "ambassadors."

2. Halfway through the weekend the students should find the time to look over their lists and make brief notes on what they have observed and what they still want to find out.

BACK IN THE CLASSROOM:

1. Discuss the homestays in a general way by starting with the students' objectives. A big chart may help focus the discussion. Have them list how completely they met their objectives under the column marked Results.

Objectives	Results
Make new friends	
Have fun and eat well	
Learn about Americans	
Practice idioms and learn slang	

2. The students list their expectations and compare them with their observations.

Expectations	Observations
American children are spoiled.	
They eat a lot of junk food.	

3. Finally, ask the students to draw conclusions and discuss what they learned.

Weekend Homestay

VARIATIONS:

1. Sometimes homestays are scheduled at the end of a language program. As a final assignment, ask the students to write you a letter about what they have learned.

2. Map-practice may be worked into the preparation. Students show where they are going and exactly how they think they will get there. A map can also be used during the follow-up to explain trips, sights seen, etc.

3. The students bring back pictures of their American families, parties, places, etc., to share.

4. Back in the classroom, see if the students can define the differences in style of hospitality between their own homes and those of their hosts. Are the differences personal or cultural? Role-plays may help. Ask the students who have had other homestays to contrast their experiences.

5. Working in small groups, the students write Mini-dramas or Role-play settings (see Language Teaching Techniques), based on their homestays. They can write home in English to tell about their weekend or write a short essay based on their experience, making a non-judgmental contrast between a specific aspect of their own and American culture.

NOTES:

1. Good sources for weekend homestays are local churches, civic organizations, and high school foreign language departments.

2. To get your "amateur anthropologists" started, there are suggestions of what to look for in the list of "Cultural Common Denominators" in "The Cultural Aspect" section of The ESL Miscellany.

Drop-Off

Fending for himself, each student is "dropped off" alone in a nearby town to explore the community by making contact with and getting help from the townspeople.

Drop-Off

PURPOSE:

An ultimate goal of language or cross-cultural study is the ability to integrate successfully into the host culture or community. This exercise approximates that experience, for students must call upon linguistic, communicative and interpersonal skills in order to learn about the origin and development of a community by meeting and enlisting the cooperation of the people of the town. Not only is the information about the town important, but the process of gathering that information and the personal experiences of each student are keys to successful exploitation of this exercise.

PREPARATION:

1. Each student's task is to chart the historical development of a town in the region. Provide general historical background by eliciting tentative answers from students through a process of guided questioning. Some sample questions:

> What was the area like before the town was founded?
>
> Why might people have started a town?
>
> What might have been some of the first buildings?
>
> What other features have been added to the town in time?

At this stage, the purpose is to raise the students' awareness of the breadth and scope of their task, giving them an idea of the kinds of data they can gather.

2. Have the students make a list of the kinds of questions they will ask.

3. Brainstorm places to go and people to seek out in a community to get answers to the questions.

4. Give the students an opportunity to talk over concerns or feelings they have about the exercise.

FIELD WORK:

1. Drive the students to towns or villages in the region, "dropping off" a student in each community.

2. Return to the communities at a pre-arranged time and place to pick up each student.

BACK IN THE CLASSROOM:

1. On the return trip and in the classroom, give the students an opportunity to discuss their affective reactions to the experience.

2. Have the students write on a piece of large paper summaries of the information they compiled.

3. Post the summaries for all to study; then have the students discuss the commonalities and differences in the summaries.

4. Ask the students for insights into American culture that they gained from the drop-off.

5. Ask your students to examine their own experience and to draw conclusions on what they learned about themselves.

Drop-Off

VARIATIONS:

1. The length of stay in the community can vary; a half-day to a full-day drop-off is effective, although the exercise can be expanded to cover a two-day period in which the students are responsible for finding food and lodging.

2. The students can be dropped off in pairs.

3. You can ask the students to write reports of their findings and experiences.

NOTES:

1. Give the students your telephone number so that they may reach you if there is a problem.

2. A valuable resource for graphically presenting the historical evolution of communities is the picture series The Changing Countryside and The Changing City by Jörg Müller.

3. To focus the gathering of information, it may be helpful to provide the students with a structural framework. One such scheme is the NAPI-KEPRA framework (Nature, Artifacts, People, Information and Kinship, Economy, Politics, Religion, Associations) explained in Guidelines for Peace Corps Cross-Cultural Training, Volume II by Albert Wright and Mary Anne Hammons.

4. Another valuable resource for the process of entering and adapting to another culture is Beyond Experience, Donald Batchelder and Elizabeth Warner, eds.

Sources and References

Batchelder, Donald; Elizabeth Warner, eds. Beyond Experience. Brattleboro, VT: Experiment Press, 1977.

Blencowe, Jacqueline W. "Activities Leading Toward Oral Fluency in the ESL Classroom." Unpublished paper, MAT Program, School for International Training.

Clark, Raymond C.; Patrick R. Moran and Arthur A. Burrows. The ESL Miscellany. Brattleboro, VT: Pro Lingua Associates, 1981.

Clark, Raymond C., ed. Index Card Games for ESL. Brattleboro, VT: Pro Lingua Associates/Experiment Press, 1982.

Clark, Raymond C. Language Teaching Techniques. Brattleboro, VT: Pro Lingua Associates, 1980.

Duncan, Janie. "Student Centered Interviews." Unpublished paper, MAT Program, The School for International Training.

Fersh, Seymour, ed. Learning About Peoples and Cultures. Evanston, IL: McDougal, Littel and Co., 1974.

Greatsinger, Calvin. Signs Around Town. Syracuse: New Readers Press, 1976.

Huizenga, Jann. Looking at American Signs. Skokie, IL: National Textbook Company.

Müller, Jörg. The Changing Countryside. New York: Atheneum Press, 1977.

Müller, Jörg. The Changing City. New York: Atheneum Press, 1977.

Richey, Jim. Sign Language. Hayward, CA: Janus, 1976.

Schumann, John. "Communication Techniques for the Intermediate and Advanced ESL Student," in Crymes, Ruth and William F. Norris, eds. On TESOL '74. Washington, DC: TESOL, 1975.

Wright, Albert; Mary Anne Hammons. Guidelines for Peace Corps Cross-Cultural Training. Volume II. Estes Park, CO: Center for Research and Education, 1970.